Driving Miss Norma

TIM BAUERSCHMIDT ♡ RAMIE LIDDLE

Driving Miss Norma

ONE FAMILY'S JOURNEY SAYING "YES" TO LIVING

HarperOne
An Imprint of HarperCollins*Publishers*

Photograph on photography-insert page 8, bottom, by Tim Bauerschmidt; page 14, top, by Patti Griest. All other photographs by Ramie Liddle.

HarperCollins books may be purchased for educational, business, or sales promotional use. For information, please email the Special Markets Department at SPsales@harpercollins.com.

FIRST EDITION

Designed by SBI Book Arts, LLC
Map illustration on pages vi and vii by David Lindroth Inc.

Library of Congress Cataloging-in-Publication Data has been applied for.

ISBN 978–0–06–266432–7

17 18 19 20 21   LSC/H   10 9 8 7 6 5 4 3 2 1

FOR MOM, DAD, AND PINKY

Contents

Driving Miss Norma

PROLOGUE

Home

BAJA CALIFORNIA, MEXICO

FEBRUARY

[Tim]

For nomads like us, home is a relative term, and ours is far off the grid on a slip of beach that separates jagged volcanic rock from the azure waters of the Sea of Cortez in Baja California, Mexico. Each winter, on this special slice of planet Earth, we unhitch our nineteen-foot Airstream trailer and temporarily come to rest.

One beautiful late February morning we hit the water early. Ringo, our seventy-three-pound Standard Poodle, sat perched at the front of my wife Ramie's paddleboard as dolphins teased him to jump off. The mist from their blowholes was backlit by the dawning sun, filling the air with a rhythm that took my breath away. I could taste the salt water on my lips from their exhalations. Ospreys and blue-footed boobies dove for their breakfasts while a whale shark filtered plankton as it passed below our boards. The sun finally revealed itself over the mountains, turning the Bay of Conception a bright, glassy gold.

Later, as we bobbed in the water with some fellow beach dwellers also taking a break from paddling, our muscles and spirits loosened and the conversation turned philosophical. The topic of aging came up, particularly the aging of our parents. We all hypothesized what we would do and how we would handle it, making plans, imagining some future way, way off.

What would Ramie and I do if her mother, Jan, in western Pennsylvania, or my parents, Leo and Norma, in northern Michigan, could no longer care for themselves? When was it time to intercede on our parents' behalf, and how? What kind of care facility was appropriate? What were their medical directives? Their hopes, their fears? Ramie's mother, so social and an avid bridge player, would probably thrive in an assisted-living situation. But my parents—who practically lived outdoors in their garden and whose lives were so predictable and so entrenched— would suffer in such a place.

In general, open roads and aging parents do not mix, which is why I had always assumed my younger sister, Stacy, would be the one who cared for them in the end. But Stacy, my only sibling, had died of cancer eight years before. "Well," Ramie said, "we don't need to figure it all out, not today. We have time. Everyone is still healthy. For now, let's just enjoy the moment." I put my fears and questions aside in favor of enjoying the moment, trusting that I had that time. Hoping that I had that time.

◊ ◊ ◊

We had not always lived on the road, although I think in one way or another this simpler, unattached lifestyle had always called out to us. When Ramie and I first met we figured out that we collectively had lived in fourteen different states. It was just synchronicity, we said, that we had wandered into the same place at the same time on the day we met.

I was a self-taught builder driving an old Ford pickup truck around the country and remodeling homes; Ramie was a non-profit consultant and had previously worked on cruise ships and at resorts in order to support her wanderlust. We had both lost close family members at an early age. Having experienced our share of grief, we were conscious of wanting to live in search of meaning rather than a paycheck. We yearned for a life lived off the beaten path, free from material things, financial burden, and even family demands.

Our lives changed forever the day Ramie's sister, Sandy, called from Maryland to offer us an old Airstream travel trailer. We were nearly two thousand miles away in Colorado and did not own a tow vehicle, but we were definitely interested. With a borrowed Chevy pickup, we drove east to see our prize. I was forty-five years old, and both Ramie and I were getting tired of tent camping and sleeping on the ground. The prospect of laying down our heads in the comfort of something with wheels was a dream come true.

The trailer was old, but it had new upholstery, a small kitchen, and a functioning toilet. I ran my hand along its weather-beaten aluminum exterior, hot from sitting out in the July sun; its iconic curves stirred a sense of anticipation in me. "This is going to be great," I told Ramie. We used the drive back to Colorado as a shakedown cruise. Our biggest decision of each day was where to park and spend the night. We felt ourselves stretching and expanding into new freedoms.

Upon our return, Ramie traded in her beloved convertible for a shiny red pickup truck with a tow package, and we were on our way to discovering a new lifestyle. We used the trailer every chance we got.

It took only one bad winter as nomads to convince us to head for warmer climes during those dark months of short days and extended nights. We had been fixing up an old fisherman's cabin in northern Michigan near my parents' house that was only intended for summer use. No matter how much hardwood we stuffed into the rusty, timeworn stove, the cabin lost the heat in a matter of hours—there was no insulation in the walls or ceiling. At night, the two of us and our dog at the time, a German shepherd named Jack, shivered together in our communal bed. I found myself dreaming of the beautiful, sunny beach where I had tent camped a few times since the mid-1990s. It was then that we settled on Mexico's Baja California Peninsula as our winter destination.

During our first season in the Baja together, we educated ourselves about the off-the-grid recreational vehicle (RV) lifestyle. We relied on a small solar panel to keep our battery lively while also conserving power use. Amps and watts and other electrical terms suddenly had relevance in our lives, a lesson we learned the hard way when our lights flickered one night and we realized we were almost out of juice.

Water conservation, too, became more important than ever since fresh water had to be hauled in from a small fishing village half an hour to the north. There was no dump station for our wastewater, so we depended on the hand-dug latrines that dotted the beach. We took showers out of a solar bag in a makeshift outdoor stall we created with a Hula-Hoop and a shower curtain balanced over an open truck door.

Despite its lack of amenities, the Baja was a magnet for a

multitude of personalities from around the world—folks like Jelle and Deb, sailors and folksingers from Canada. For them, home in the summer is a sailboat anchored in Maple Bay off Vancouver Island. Winters are spent on Baja California beaches in a thirteen-foot vintage travel trailer with no bathroom. Chris and Bessy, retired computer programmers who once lived in South Africa, now split time between upstate New York, San Francisco, and the Baja. There was "Santa Wayne," British Columbia's best-loved Santa Claus impersonator. He did not arrive at the beach until after Christmas, for obvious reasons. And who could forget Pedro and Janet, the colorful international ring-master for equestrian show-jumping events and his Dutch-born horse-trainer wife? Pedro did not leave his flamboyant style behind just because he was at the beach. These regulars, the ones who came back year after year, were mainly North Americans, but many other foreign travelers passed through on their way to mainland Mexico via the ferry in La Paz, located farther south.

Our days always started with an early kayak paddle around the nearest island, located one mile offshore. We would float and wait for the sun to rise over the mountainous peninsula that formed the bay, rejoicing in the stillness of the morning before returning to shore. We would grab a quick breakfast of locally grown strawberries over yogurt before joining a group for our three-mile walk up the hill and then down a windy desert trail back to the bay. After getting the local beach gossip on the way to our trailer, we would decide what else to do that day—paddleboarding, swimming, a longer hike, or perhaps visiting friends new and old.

Everyone avoided talking about politics and religion, and eschewed news from the outside world, even if it was just for the four or five winter months each year. We connected with these like-minded beach dwellers. While both Ramie and I found it difficult to maintain friendships in the many towns and neighborhoods where we had lived, here it was different. Here, where there was no traffic, no news, no external clock to watch, people could go about the business of just being—with the earth, with one another, with themselves. We felt like we truly belonged.

We spent two of the three winters we owned the lake cabin on our half-mile crescent of sand in the Baja. When we sold the cabin, we bought a larger Airstream and spent the following winter in Florida while Ramie earned a postgraduate degree in school counseling. We traveled to Colorado for her internship and then parked in Prescott, Arizona, living in our trailer until we found a home there to renovate.

While the larger trailer was more than adequate to live in, we wanted to travel, explore, and feel closer to the natural world. We found ourselves staying home more because it was too much of an effort to drag the behemoth around. Realizing the problem, Ramie and I decided to downsize to a nineteen-foot Airstream Bambi. This worked better for us, and we then traveled for months at a time, usually in the "shoulder season" when school was in session and families generally stayed home. The national parks and other attractions were less crowded during these times. Our road trips, now with our new puppy Ringo along, grew longer and longer—whole summers, six months, and even more.

We were gone so much that our Arizona home was empty most of the time. When Ramie was working, we traveled during school breaks around the Southwest, exploring places like the north rim of the Grand Canyon, Death Valley, and Bryce Canyon and Zion National Parks. In the summers, we visited friends in Tennessee and North Carolina, and dropped in on Sandy, the one who started it all, in southern Maryland. Northern Michigan was always a stop whenever we went back east.

In 2011, during a yearlong sabbatical, we spanned the country from coast to coast and north to south. We left Arizona and traveled north through Nevada's Great Basin, on to Idaho's Sawtooth Mountains and then Glacier National Park in Montana. From there, we traveled west and followed the Oregon coast south, continuing along California's coastal Highway 1 until we reached the Mexican border. After wintering in the Baja, we spent spring and summer traveling east across the southern tier of states and then north all the way to Maine before turning back toward Arizona.

We loved to nestle our little Bambi between the boulders of Utah's Arches National Park and hike early in the morning before the crowds and heat arrived, or park in a secluded grove of redwood trees in Northern California and sleep under the thousand-year-old canopy and even older stars.

We made friends at familiar stops and headed for places where our Baja California friends lived. In Avery, California, we stayed on John and Lori's land, high in the Sierra Nevada, parked on a flat spot in the canyon that follows Love Creek. One year we arrived during apple harvest season, so we rolled up our sleeves and helped process more than two hundred pounds of apples the old-fashioned way—with a heavy cast-iron grinder and a slatted hardwood press—before filtering and then funneling the sweet juice into bottles.

One Easter we had returned to Arizona, and because we had rented out our Prescott home, we had parked on our friend Kasie's thirty-eight-acre horse ranch in Williamson Valley. Early that Sunday morning, Kasie strolled up to our Airstream and asked for our help with something. Much to our surprise, our time there coincided with breeding season for her magnificent stallion, Morgan, and before we knew it, we were helping assemble, operate, and regulate the temperature of a brand-new artificial equine vagina.

We worked on being more flexible, and we became more forgiving of ourselves and of others on the road. We did not have much choice, really; orchestrating our travel plans around free dump stations (which our GPS sometimes failed to locate) and travel delays in small towns (whether due to a parade, a marathon, or road construction) sort of demanded an open mind and a free spirit. There was also the catalog of things we inevitably forgot at home, which forced us to come up with innovative solutions to accomplish certain tasks. Not to mention our encounters with coyote pups, moose, bears, migrating butterflies, and a woman in high heels walking her pet pig along the campground loop and wearing a monogrammed sweater that matched the one worn by her pig. No matter how seasoned you are or how much you plan, travel teaches you to expect the unexpected and to roll with it.

Of course we got road weary, but for us it was worth it. Embracing ridiculous and often disrupted plans meant we were also open to experiences that otherwise would have passed us by. Some nights we were woken up by the sound of salmon spawning just feet from our bedroom window; on others we found ourselves midnight paddleboarding, still energized by the sight of a full moon. Thwarted travel plans might mean another day spent feeling the lightness and smallness of our beings under the expansive, deep blue sky of the American West. Spontaneous supply runs could make us feel giddy and childlike, inspiring Ramie to stand on the back rail of a shopping cart filled with groceries as I pushed her at a full run through the parking lot back to our trailer, a note of pure exhilaration in her laughter.

There was a simplicity to life on the road, a freedom that Ramie and I felt was an antidote to the angst of modern life. The less we owned and the less we owed, the less we worried. Waking and sleeping not according to a clock but to the sun's rising and setting; hiking, playing, reading, and eating in tune with our own rhythms—this was, and still is, the beauty of our nomadic life.

We were like reeds blowing in the wind, living free and traveling light, with the Baja as our lodestar. The unexpected acquisition of the Airstream had saved our lives—or, more accurately, it had taught us how to truly live our lives: eyes and hearts wide open to whatever life had to offer.

◊ ◊ ◊

Ramie and I had had fifteen opportunities to talk to my parents about their wishes. That is the number of times Ramie had joined me on my yearly pilgrimages to their rural Michigan home. The first year she came with me, Mom and Dad were in their mid-seventies—perhaps a little too young then to have this talk. Honestly it never dawned on us. They were still very self-sufficient and vibrant, after all. But as they aged into their eighties, I began to see a shift in my parents' capabilities. They moved slower. Mom could not manage the stairs to the basement anymore, so Dad had to do the laundry. Cooking healthy meals became a hassle for Mom. Getting the mail from the box across the street became more of a chore for Dad. But they soldiered on.

We would do our best to help them out in the week or so we visited. I would work on the deferred household maintenance while Ramie shaped up the yard. I removed loose rugs and installed smoke/CO detectors. I installed rails and grab bars. I made a year's worth of dinners and froze them in the upright freezer I brought up from the basement. I did everything but have "the talk."

◊ ◊ ◊

Our time in the Baja was growing short, and the spring season of departures was upon us. Some folks had already packed up and moved on. Those who were uncomfortable with good-byes usually just drove away, quietly sneaking out; others might hear Pedro blow his bugle and then leave in a parade-like fashion. Each departure was as unique as the individuals camped in our community.

In a few short weeks, Ramie and I would start packing up too. We would rinse the salt water off our beach toys, hoist them onto the roof racks, and tie them down. The hammock would come down from the *palapa,* and the screen tent would be folded up and packed in its bag. As best as we could, we would sweep the sand out of the trailer and the truck, knowing it was impossible to leave it all behind.

And then we would travel north on Mexico Highway 1 up the mountainous peninsula, through the Baja wine country, to the U.S. border crossing at Tecate as we began our annual five-thousand-mile lumbering journey east, across the country, visiting friends and family, and eventually all the way to the tip of northern Michigan again to see my mom and dad. Although we had no idea, we were in for a rude awakening.

CHAPTER 1

Priorities

PRESQUE ISLE, MICHIGAN

JUNE

[Ramie]

Life is fragile. We all say that, but most of the time the truth of it does not move from our head to our heart. We take people for granted, ignore aches and pains, do not say the things that we know we need to say, putting them off for a later time. And what Tim and I were continually putting off was this: talking to his parents about aging, and particularly how they wanted to live the ends of their lives. Why was this topic so hard to bring up? Why had we continually chickened out, the questions we wanted to ask remaining stuck in our throats? What would we do when that moment came and we had no choice but to face their mortality—and ours? Was there a way to say "Yes" to living even as we looked death in the face?

It was with firm resolve to address some of these questions that we pulled into the driveway of my in-laws' Presque Isle,

Michigan, home for our annual visit. We were determined that this was going to be the year we finally found the strength to broach the subject, but as is so often the case, a crisis hit us before we had time to do any talking.

Tim's mother, Norma, usually greeted us, letting us know what kind of cookies she had baked for us. Tim's father, Leo, often helped him park the trailer. But during the time it took us to back up the Airstream along the south side of the asphalt driveway, neither had emerged from their small brick home.

We did not need to say it to each other, but we were both worried.

Walking swiftly, we climbed the handful of steps that led to the side entrance, opened the door, and proceeded through the mudroom and into the eat-in kitchen. Something was burning.

And something was wrong—very, very wrong.

"Mom? Dad?"

No one answered.

Tim switched off the oven without looking to see what was in it.

One of Leo's many clocks began to chime, out of sync with the real time, then another and another. The grandfather clock, the one Leo meticulously wound every Sunday, was idle. A NASCAR event blared from the living room television, but the chairs where Leo and Norma usually sat were empty. We made our way to the back of the house.

That was when we saw them in the hall, making their way toward us from the bathroom.

At first sight, nothing appeared awry. But then we noticed that Leo was hunched forward, with his arm around Norma's shoulder, his face contorted in pain. My tiny mother-in-law strained to hold him up, balancing herself with a cane in her left hand.

They inched toward us. With each step, Leo cried out, not acknowledging us.

We rushed forward. Tim wrapped his arm around him. I did the same with Norma.

"Mom, what happened?"

"Dad, talk to me. What's going on?"

"When did this happen?"

"Watch the rug! Pick up your feet."

"Hang on to me."

"Dad, I got you."

"Everything is going to be okay."

"Let's get you in your chair."

With Leo whimpering and wincing, we shuffled toward the living room. Quickly, I settled Norma into her chair, but it took more effort and much more time to settle Leo into his. Another clock chimed when it should not have. The television continued to roar. I grabbed the remote, fumbling with it; it was unfamiliar to me. Where was the mute button? Finally, the television went silent.

Normally a happy, jovial guy, Leo moaned and, at times, wailed. We brought him pillows and helped him shift positions, but none of it relieved his agonizing pain. Tim and Norma retreated to the kitchen, where they talked quietly. I hovered near Leo, hoping against hope that I could find a way to make him comfortable.

Leo looked up at me and said, "Something is really f*cked up."

In all my years of knowing him, he had never used such language in my presence. Those few words told me all I needed to know.

When Tim returned from the kitchen, he told me he had looked in the oven and had found a small, unseasoned piece of chicken and two shriveled potatoes on a foil tray. *That was all they were eating for supper?*

A knot of anxiety filled my chest. This was not over by any stretch. It was just the beginning.

◊ ◊ ◊

Months before our visit, our biggest daily decision had been whether we should paddle our boards or our kayaks, go swimming . . . or do all three. Each day the sun had warmed and bronzed our skin, and our warmhearted companions, the breathtaking scenery, the fresh seafood, and the mariachi music had conspired to make every day perfect.

After leaving Mexico that spring, we traveled back to the States through California and then east to Tennessee, staying in the parking lots of a string of Cracker Barrel restaurants and Walmart Supercenters. Along the way, we occasionally called and asked Norma and Leo how they were doing. They never mentioned needing any support, although they probably would not ask for help even if they did, and we never pursued it. As Tim said, "No news is good news."

Eventually, we landed in North Carolina, staying with our friends Caroline and Roland on their beautiful thirty-five-acre farm, complete with stunning gardens, grazing horses, and several outbuildings. Ringo loved to run around the property with the two resident dogs. I had been battling a fever for several days by then. I felt lousy, and I was looking for something, anything, to take my mind off how sick I was. So while everyone else was enjoying each other's company, I decided to stay in bed with a book.

Several of the farm's outbuildings housed libraries, all of them with floor-to-ceiling bookshelves; I had thousands of options to choose from. I was too sick to leave the guesthouse, so I shuffled through the bookshelves there without finding one that interested me. Then I came across a short stack of books perched on a small antique table in the hall. One title caught my eye—*Being Mortal: Medicine and What Matters in the End* by Atul Gawande, a critical examination of end-of-life medical care. I was feeling particularly mortal in that moment, so I slid it out from the middle of the stack and carried it back to bed.

A few days later, I was almost done reading the book. I was not feeling better physically, but I knew my life had changed. What I had just read was important stuff. The way I looked at the end of life had been flipped upside down and backward. My head had been stuck in the sand when it came to talking about the needs of my own mom and Tim's parents, but I knew now that it was time to have those tough conversations.

From the farm, we headed to North Carolina's Outer Banks. We were waiting for the ferry from Ocracoke to Cape Hatteras when Tim's cell phone rang.

The caller was Leo, telling us that Tim's uncle Ralph—Leo's best friend and Norma's last remaining sibling—had just died at age ninety-one.

Leo's voice sounded strong that day, but just a few weeks later on Father's Day, when we talked to him again on the phone, it had changed.

"We have to go," Tim said after he ended the call. "Something's wrong with my dad."

What I am most struck by now, when I think back on the months before that phone call, is this: the audacity of our assumption of control. The thing about aging and illness is that they care very little for our plans; both unfold in their own time, whether we are ready to face these inevitable issues or not.

◊ ◊ ◊

We never even had time to unhitch our Airstream from the truck. Three days after we had pulled into the driveway, Leo lay on his side in the fetal position in a hospital bed, his organs failing. The Fentanyl patches he was using to control his unbearable back pain—the result of what we eventually learned was a compression fracture—apparently pushed his body chemistry out of whack, and the doctors could not bring it back to order. He appeared so uncomfortable and alone. Norma was smaller than she had ever looked, dwarfed by the reclining hospital chair next to Leo's bed. She was silent.

Tim crawled into bed with his dad, spooning him. I handed him a damp cloth, and he used it to gently wipe Leo's brow. Repeatedly, Tim told him, "It's okay, I'm going to take care of Mom. I love you. Everything is going to be okay."

After some time, Tim took a break and I crawled into the bed with Leo. We did this off and on that morning until Norma whispered to me, "Can you take me downstairs? I have an appointment at one o'clock for some tests."

I had no idea what the tests were for. In the elevator on the way down, she mentioned she had had some blood in her urine. I suspected there was more to it than that because I also noticed the sanitary pads tucked in her purse. Clearly she was bleeding, and having reached menopause decades before, she should not have been. I stayed in the waiting room, and when she emerged from her tests, we returned to Leo's room. Norma made no mention of the procedure. In that moment our priority was Leo, so Tim and I did not push the issue with her.

As the week progressed, we learned that Norma needed follow-up testing, including a transvaginal ultrasound. With her husband dying just a couple of floors above her in the hospital's hospice wing, Norma lay on a paper-covered table while a technician inserted an ultrasound wand. Her entire body seemed to contract inward. She was small, and humiliated. I stood near the technician and watched as she circled the display screen over and over again with a stylus and saw what looked to be a large mass on Norma's uterus. "Unbelievable," I murmured to myself. Here Leo was dying, and from what I was seeing on the screen, Norma had something that looked like a tumor. From her vantage point, Norma could not see what was going on and was unaware of what I had just seen.

I took a deep breath before I told Tim what had appeared on the monitor that afternoon.

Leo was soon transferred to a hospice room in a local nursing home. Two days later, after we had sat at his bedside for six hours, an exhausted Norma insisted that he was well taken care of by his faith. "We can leave now," she said. We all left knowing that this warm July day would be Leo's last. No sooner had we returned home than we got a call from hospice telling us that he had died at 5:50 P.M. Right at that moment, a broken ship's clock—a gift to Leo from Stacy—started ticking again.

We had Leo's remains cremated, and we buried his urn next to Stacy's in the family plot a few paces from Uncle Ralph at the township cemetery. We were in shock and grieving.

It was not yet official, but Tim and I also knew in our hearts that Norma likely had cancer. As we lay in bed in the Airstream, we talked about our options. Neither of us wanted the same ending for Norma as we had seen Leo experience. His last days in a busy, noisy hospital were far from pleasant. In fact, they were excruciating for him. We both worried about what would happen if Norma went into a nursing home. She loved being outdoors. How would she exist inside a facility with a locked front door that required a code to get out? How could this very shy woman ever share a room with a stranger? We had seen the institutional food served in many of these places. There was no assurance she would have the quality or variety of life she was used to, nor the independence or anything that was familiar to her. Our intuition told us that Norma not only needed but also deserved freedom, autonomy, and dignity, and to us, the nursing homes we had access to represented the opposite of those values.

If Norma wanted to kick back at the end of the day with a beer or a glass of wine, we wanted her to have that luxury. If she wanted to leave the facility for any reason, we wanted her to be able to do it. If she wanted to eat breakfast for dinner or walk barefoot in the grass, so be it. We also wanted her to have the chance to smile again.

We looked at each other and, simultaneously, we said, "We need to see if she wants to come along."

We had no idea what we would do if she said "Yes."

◊ ◊ ◊

The following day, the three of us sat down at the kitchen table to have some lunch.

"Norma, we don't know what the doctor is going to say about all the tests they have been doing," I said between bites, "but I'm wondering how you are feeling about how you might take care of yourself now that Leo is gone."

"I don't know what to do," she said, sounding feebler with each word. "I can't live here by myself. I know that."

Tim chimed in, "Well, Ramie and I have been talking about that too, and we wouldn't feel good about you staying here by yourself even if you had people helping you. We looked into homes and we can get you on a list either here or where Ramie's mom lives in Pennsylvania.

"Or, we were thinking," he continued, "if you would like to live with us on the road, we could get a bigger RV."

"While coming with us might seem like a crazy idea," I interjected, "it's no crazier than spending the rest of your days in a nursing home. If you want to come, we'll take you anywhere you want to go."

We told her she did not have to give us an answer right away. "Just think about it," we said.

We continued to eat our ham-salad sandwiches without conversation.

The next person to speak was Norma. She quietly said, "I think I'd like to come along."

The next morning, we sat crammed in a small examination room with a gynecologist and a medical student shadowing him. We had spent the past two days after Leo's death moving from doctor to doctor and from test to test. The ob-gyn was the last one to see.

A handsome man in his thirties, the doctor told us what we already knew: Norma had a cancerous mass on her uterus. From his perch on the edge of the exam table, he looked down at Norma, who was sitting in a hospital wheelchair, and then launched into an assumed close: "So we're going to schedule you for a hysterectomy, then radiation and chemotherapy. You will recover in a rehabilitation facility, and it will likely take a few months to heal."

Although he gave Norma no other options, he finished by asking what she would like to do. She locked eyes with him and, with as much conviction as she could muster, said, "I'm ninety years old. I'm hitting the road."

With good reason, the doctor appeared confused. Tim explained that we lived on the road in an RV and that we planned to take Norma along with us for as long as she was interested and physically able.

The doctor's demeanor shifted instantly. He lit up. The medical student seemed amazed—this response was probably not what she had expected from this tiny old woman.

"Are we being irresponsible?" Tim asked. "This approach seems perfectly natural to us, but we don't always live within the rules. What do you think?"

"No," the doctor said, "it is not irresponsible. There's no guarantee that at her age she'd survive the surgery. If she did, she would be in intensive care and dealing with miserable side effects. As doctors, we see the other side of this every day. If it were me in this situation, I'd want to be in that motor home."

"Right on," Tim and I replied.

We had a lot to accomplish in order to fulfill our promise to take Norma on one last adventure. To begin with, we had no idea how long this adventure would last or even where it would take us. But we knew that we had to try.

CHAPTER 2

Exploration

NORTHERN MICHIGAN

AUGUST

[*Tim*]

The days after Dad's death were full of grief and planning, a delicate meeting of endings and beginnings. His death punctured the pace of each day as loss so often does, and my mom's terminal diagnosis quickly redefined time as something we were running out of. Had I said all the things I had wanted or needed to say to my dad before he died? I do not believe that I had. Had he felt my love and gratitude for him? I like to believe that he did, as I whispered those words into his ear as he lay in his hospital bed. My dad was gone and my mom was dying; suddenly, after years of a relationship defined by annual visits and irregular phone calls, the three of us were going to live together in a home on wheels. This would certainly be my last chance to share any personal feelings with my mom. I did not want to be asking myself the same questions about my mom as I had about my dad. I wanted to be sure this time.

"I think I'd like to come along," Mom had said. It was as simple as that. And in the space of a breath, we began to plan a road trip with my frail, grieving mom, knowing that our lives would be utterly transformed.

I was fifty-seven years old. I had spent the past fifteen years living on and off the grid, blissfully—and sometimes ridiculously—detached. It was just me, Ramie, and more recently Ringo. Now I was going to be a caregiver, the codirector of a mobile assisted-living home. Although I saw no other way to take good care of Mom, I still was not sure that I could really pull this off, or what kind of strain the arrangement might put on my marriage.

Grief formed above all of us like a thick, dark cloud. When I was overwhelmed by the feeling, I would lie on the floor of the Airstream—which was still parked in my parents' driveway—and with my arms clutching Ringo's soft, dense curls, I would sob until exhaustion gave me reprieve and I could sleep. But Ramie and I did not share our grief or our fears. We did not sit around the dinner table with my mom and reminisce. Instead, we packed.

Our plan was to travel together for a year with Mom. After that, we would reassess the situation. In truth, we did not believe she would live through the year, but we hoped that by setting a goal, her desire to continue living would increase. We had a lot to buy and do in the next five weeks before we could go. Mom needed assistance getting around, so we bought her a lightweight, ergonomic wheelchair. Although she was still able to walk with a cane, we could transport her more swiftly in her new Karma wheelchair, which also served as a "walker." We also had to settle Dad's estate and help Mom pack, but first we needed to figure out a budget that worked for everyone.

Ramie and I had been able to retire early because of many years of frugal living, our lack of debt, and forgoing having a family. We always drove older vehicles and almost never splurged while we were on the road. We would primarily stay at low-cost campsites without full hookups or we would "dry camp" in a chain-store parking lot or on public land. We took a small yearly stipend out of our investments and lived off that. We had enough money in our budget to continue to do this even with my mom now on board, taking care of all our own expenses plus Mom's food. For the additional comforts Mom required—some nicer campgrounds with full hookups, a more comfortable living arrangement, and an occasional meal out (all things we avoided when it was just us)—we would dedicate Mom's social security income and the small pension left by Dad.

We did some research regarding the cost of nursing home care, and near my mom's home it was $8,400 per month for a shared room. That was about $280 a day. None of our cost calculations for living with her on board came anywhere near that amount. In fact, every day Mom stayed out of a nursing home would allow us to use the financial legacy my dad had left behind on a higher quality of life for her. Instead of a non-refundable buy-in at a nursing home, which we found could cost upward of $120,000, we would invest in a larger motor home, which could be resold and the money used to care for Mom when our journey ended.

The next order of business, then, was to find a motor home that would work for all of us. While Ramie and I actually got a kick out of showering in our RV while in a Walmart parking lot and depended on only solar power for our reading lights, we knew my mom would require a few more creature comforts.

At the old oak table in Mom's kitchen, over another ham-salad sandwich, the three of us talked about what we would need in a motor home to make our plan work. A comfortable chair for Mom was high on the list, along with two private sleeping areas and a bathroom in the center of the coach so we did not have to cross into each other's space. "How are we going to do laundry?" Mom asked. We added a washer and dryer to our list. "We need a floor plan that allows Norma to walk through the motor home," Ramie pointed out, leaning over her laptop, Internet browser open. Layouts with L-shaped couches, small doorways, and kitchen islands were crossed out. Let us not make a television the focus of our attention, we all agreed. And no need for a fireplace. Every detail mattered to us; things like privacy and the right kind of communal space were now major concerns.

And then we found it: a motor-home layout that included a bath and a half, a washer/dryer combo, and a Euro-style chair—the Fleetwood Southwind 36D.

We sifted through every used-RV outlet we could find on the Internet, searching for a Southwind we could afford on our budget. There were nine for sale in various parts of the country. One by one, we eliminated the options. Some were too far away, others too expensive, still others had too-high mileage, but one was just right. It was in upstate New York, about nine hundred miles away from Mom's home. It was perfect. Sight unseen, we put down a large deposit.

Well, perfect except for one big problem: my plan to drive Dad's Jeep Patriot to New York and tow it back to Michigan was not going to work. The Patriot could not be flat-towed behind a motor home because of its transmission. It appeared that we now needed a new car too. And the only one that would work for us was another Jeep model, the Wrangler.

After a few dead ends, Ramie found a Jeep dealership in Cheboygan, Michigan. Lenny, the sales manager, told us he had two Jeeps on his lot that might work but warned that one was tricked out with thirty-thousand dollars' worth of aftermarket bling. In reality, there was only one option on his lot. We decided to make the ninety-minute ride from Mom's house to take a test-drive anyway.

On a clear, sunny July day, Ramie and I set out for the dealership in the supercharged Toyota MR2 that Stacy had gifted to my dad several years before. Ramie, strapped into the bucket seat next to me, was studying the puffy white clouds through the open T-top as we followed the two-lane highway north. "Are you sleeping on this beautiful ride?" I asked her after we were about halfway there.

"Nope," she said, her presence feeling relaxed for the first time since we had arrived at my parents' place.

"Then what are you doing?" I inquired.

"Talking to Stacy," she replied matter-of-factly.

In the midst of finding a new motor home and tow vehicle, we had also been struggling to find a place for us to winter in Florida. Although it was only July, every RV park we had contacted was booked. It was almost as if the Sunshine State had put up a NO VACANCY sign for the season.

"I'm asking Stacy to find us a great campsite in Florida and for the perfect car to show up without any hassle," Ramie added.

We arrived about forty-five minutes later to meet Lenny in front of the dealership's fancy glass showroom. A small man not much larger than Mom, with a happy skip in his step and a quick smile, Lenny rushed toward us. "Ramie!" he said. "You aren't going to believe this! Just over a half hour ago a new four-door Jeep Wrangler came in on dealer trade. I had no idea it was coming. I think it is exactly what you are looking for."

He was half right: it was perfect, but we *did* believe it. It was just the sign from above that we needed. Perhaps we felt a little powerful in that moment too. We were bucking the system and no one—neither doctors nor car salesmen—were trying to talk us out of it. This audacious plan just might work, we thought.

But would Mom be able to climb into the backseat of the Jeep?

A few days later, Ramie and I trekked back to Cheboygan, this time with Mom and Ringo in tow.

"Wow! That's what we're buying? Pretty nice," I overheard Mom whisper to Ramie. I laughed to myself at her excitement over a vehicle that looked fit for a safari in contrast to the tan Buick sedans that dominated the parking lots and driveways of northern Michigan.

Right away it was clear that Mom's legs were not long enough or strong enough to climb in. Lenny searched around for a step stool, and soon Mom was sitting tall in the backseat next to her pal Ringo.

Lenny enthused, "What do you think?"

Mom, normally quiet and reserved, surprised us all when she quipped back, "Lenny, I'll tell you what. This is a very nice car. There are only two problems with it."

Lenny, anxious to make the sale, said, "What could be wrong?"

"Well, I can't get in it, and I can't get out of it. If you throw in the step stool, you've got yourself a deal."

We signed the papers for our new Jeep Wrangler that day. Soon I was on my way to pick up our new motor home, full of grateful determination.

◊ ◊ ◊

I took a deep breath and got up to stretch my legs. There had been a break in the August heat, and this day was cool and breezy. I walked around to the back of the house, pausing at Mom's garden, which was already showing signs of wildness from lack of human intervention. Weeds wrapped their way around the tall, scraggly tomato plants. Herbs grew bushy and knee-high and had gone to seed, too late for harvesting now. Ringo lounged on his belly and rubbed his nose in the tall grass. The slightly mildewy smell of my parents' midwestern basement, where I had spent the morning going through some of their stuff, had seeped into my bones, clinging to my clothes even out here in the open air.

Back in the house, I found most of my father's papers organized with an almost obsessive neatness in a wooden filing cabinet stored in a spare bedroom. Thick files protected owner's manuals and warranty information for items that had long since been decomposing in a landfill.

Everything was categorized and well thought out, just as I had known my dad to be—no mess, no drama. I had never seen my parents fight or cry; I had never seen them ecstatically happy either. We had not talked about money matters, much in the same way we had not talked about health matters.

One recent day, when I had been sifting through my parents' financial documents, something fluttered to the floor. I bent and reached for it: a newspaper clipping advertising for hot-air balloon rides on the other side of the state. Later, as I opened the door to grab a cold drink, I noticed another one held to the refrigerator by a magnet. Then I discovered yet another, serving as a makeshift page marker in a book. "Dad and I always wanted to go hot-air ballooning," Mom revealed after I questioned her about my finds, "but we never made it." I felt deflated, and also a little stunned. My parents had wanted to do this—this bold and adventurous thing? It did not seem real to me.

How well did I really know them? Like most children, I could describe my parents in great detail. They were so predictable, Ramie and I joked that we always knew what they were doing, even when we were miles away. They ate lunchmeat sandwiches with potato chips and dill pickles every day at noon. They took a nap in their respective lounge chairs after reading the day's mail at one o'clock. Dinner was always at five thirty. They were in bed after the ten o'clock news broadcast.

For the nearly seven decades my folks had been together, Dad was the front man, always ready with a smile and a bad joke. He was funny, sociable, and quick to engage; Mom never really had to talk as long as Dad was around. She could smile and laugh at his jokes, and she mastered facial expressions that would complement his silly stories. It seemed to me that she had gone most of her life without engaging with others in her own voice. I assumed it had been her choice, that she preferred to laugh and observe.

Yet there was my mom, all spunky and coy, teasing Lenny at the car dealership. And here, trailed across the house, was a romantic dream of my dad and mom's. Yes, I knew my parents, but there were also so many blanks to be filled in. Was there a side to my mom that she had kept hidden all these years? What other roads had she and Dad not taken? What did Mom miss about my sister, Stacy? About Dad? I craved answers, to break through the stoic facade of parental distance I had known all my life.

Ramie helped Mom pack her things and I prepared essentials for the motor home. Among the items my mom gathered to fill her two allotted drawers was a faded red pullover sweatshirt from a rustic lakeside resort down the road, the Fireside Inn.

"Why would she bring this old thing?" I asked Ramie. "She knows space is limited, right?"

"It's a symbol of her past," Ramie reflected, "a part of her grieving process."

Ramie was right. She and I were used to traveling light and planning little. I could already tell that this journey was to be different.

Packing and planning underscored Mom's loss in ways that none of us yet had words for. No longer would she inhabit a home full of possessions that meant so much to her and Dad, nor would she perform the daily rituals they had developed over sixty-seven years of marriage. She would no longer sleep in her own bed, the one that still remembered the weight of Dad's body and held the pillow that still smelled of him. She had lost her last and closest sibling, my uncle Ralph, just one month before. She had outlived all her peers and was the last of her generation.

My mom did not cry. She was steadfast in her faith. She had been raised in a staunch and stoic German household. She had survived the Great Depression.

But her grief manifested itself in physical ways. She had lost her appetite—what little there was—and she was losing weight. Mom seemed to be shrinking in size right before our eyes. She was quieter than usual. She seemed confused, and I remember her saying to us, "What am I going to do now?" Grief and illness consumed her, but still she did not cry.

Her decision to join us on the road seemed to be an expression of her optimism, her way of saying, *"I'm not done yet; I still have fun and curiosity left in me."* Although my mom owned plenty of nice clothes, she was excited to buy new ones for the trip, and Ramie and I were delighted and encouraged by her enthusiasm. We asked if she wanted to bring anything from her house along. "Only one thing," she said. "The two throw pillows from the couch." That was probably more out of practicality (we needed some) than nostalgia.

"Do you want to bring any photos of Dad or Stacy?" we asked.

"No."

We brought along a family snapshot from our wedding in case she changed her mind.

In place of nostalgic items, she chose to load up on books and jigsaw puzzles for the road. In fact, the very first item she slipped into her bag was a pair of binoculars, soon followed by several field guides to study the natural world along the way. We restrung her dulcimer, tucked in her sketch pads, and found a spot to safely store her knitting needles. We gave her an old iPad to play solitaire and word games on, which she learned to use thanks to Ramie's patience.

Despite spending the last twenty-eight years there, my mom was not sentimental about leaving the house. We decided to leave it just as it was until some other time; we wanted her to spend her energy on truly living, not on divesting herself of possessions. She did not want to have to deal with them and neither did we. We would drain the pipes and close the house up without giving it a final cleaning, unsure if Mom would even be alive when we planned to return the following year.

Ramie placed a road atlas next to Mom, seated in her rocking chair in the living room, and pulled out her regional Smithsonian travel books from the bookshelf in the back room—she had the whole set.

"You can go anywhere in the country," we told her.

"Oh . . . I don't know. It all seems nice. I would like to see it all."

We persisted.

"I always wanted to spend time in New Mexico," she admitted one day. "I don't know why, but I always wanted to go there." At least it was a start. "And I would like to see the presidents' heads at Mount Rushmore," she later added. "That would be nice."

Meanwhile, Mom had dropped from her already slight 101 pounds to a fragile 94. She was frail, dizzy, lethargic, and nearly wordless, as if she had completely run out of things to say. We could still see a spark in her, but we saw the depths of her grief and the effects of illness and her medications written on her body and spirit too. Our journey held so much promise. With extended time to talk, I would now have the opportunity to ask her questions, hear a few answers, and perhaps discover who my mom really was. I said a silent prayer that she would remain well enough to tell me.

Then, finally, it was time to go. On a sunny August morning, we pulled out of the driveway and started for the highway. We were heading to Mount Rushmore National Memorial in South Dakota. When I glanced at Ramie, I knew I did not need to ask. She and I were both breathing a sigh of relief.

CHAPTER 3

Discovery

THE HEARTLAND

AUGUST

[Ramie]

We drove two hours that first day. Simply getting out of the driveway while Norma was still alive was an accomplishment, we thought. We hitched up the Jeep behind the motor home in the parking lot of the local township hall, and then I watched Norma's face as we drove past the house she had called home for almost thirty years.

She sat buckled into the dining table seat facing forward, the spot that gave the best view out all the windows. She seemed pensive as she studied the trees she and Leo had planted in their yard over the years. We had not told any of her friends about the cancer diagnosis. Norma did not want to see the look in their eyes—it did not make sense for them to worry—but it was front and center on our minds as we pulled away.

Only minutes before, Norma had said good-bye to her few remaining longtime friends and neighbors, her unemotional German face intact as she waved and watched some of them weep. Now it was just us. Everything else had been peeled away. Here we were, Tim, Ringo, and I, taking a fragile old woman on a seemingly aimless journey. I could not help but wonder if she would ever see her beautiful perennial garden again or tend to the rows of lavender that filled the air with the scent of southern France when they were in bloom. If I were a gambler, I would have bet that same thought was going through her mind too. Of course she would never speak of it. Her hands were folded neatly on the dining table, and even though her cloudy eyes betrayed the tumult of the past weeks, her pink lips were sealed as she embarked on the next chapter of her long life.

As we meandered north along the Lake Huron shoreline, I noticed with surprise the faraway horizon. Miles and miles of rippling blue water extended infinitely into the bright sky. I suddenly had a fresh perspective—when driving in a passenger car so low to the ground I could never see over the stunted trees that typically lined the roads of northern Michigan. Sitting high in our new motor home, we had a new vantage point.

The view from our giant front windshield was now our window to the world. It dawned on me that although Tim and I had zigzagged across this country many times, we were going to have a chance to see it through a different lens this time. A few lenses, really: the motor home's huge windshield and the eyes of a ninety-year-old woman who had the strength to say "Yes" to adventure.

After that first day on the road, I reveled in the novelty of having ice cubes in our motor home's freezer, a luxury we had not known in our Airstream. Tim and Norma enjoyed a cold beer before dinner, and we all toasted to a successful maiden voyage. Norma took her first RV shower, flushed her first vacuum-style toilet (or at least tried to), and spent her first night of blissful sleep in her new Sleep Number bed set at a cozy number 40.

On the other side of the sliding bedroom door, we endured a restless night in our new sleeping quarters—complete with a steering wheel and kitchen sink—on a couch with a double air mattress that we had to make up every night. Ringo slept on the floor near the dinette table.

The freedom Tim and I had worked our whole lives to achieve was somehow still intact, yet in very practical terms we had completely lost it. With Tim's every toss and turn on the inflatable bed, I was rolled awake. I really had no idea how we would manage this.

◊ ◊ ◊

The next day we were poised to cross the Mackinac Bridge, the longest suspension bridge in the world. "Big Mac" connects Michigan's lower and upper peninsulas and is where Lake Huron gives Lake Michigan a big sloppy kiss.

The trees were blowing sideways—not a good sign for a day when we planned to traverse the watery connection between two Great Lakes. Eventually, high wind warnings closed the famous bridge to "high profile" vehicles similar to ours. Like it or not, we were forced to sit tight in the campground that overlooked the Straits of Mackinac.

A chilly, misty rain descended upon us. Late August suddenly felt more like late autumn, and I suddenly felt profoundly alone in the world. When it was just Tim and me traveling, we could always count on each other for conversation, entertainment, food preparation, and canine care. Now one or the other of us was always preoccupied with his mom's needs.

Norma was easy to be around, and she had made it clear from the beginning that she did not want to be a burden, yet in my every moment I was concerned about her comfort. Was she in pain? Was she bored? Was she drinking enough water? How could we get her to eat? She really could not afford to lose any more weight.

Before leaving the safety of Norma's driveway, I had outlined our next four months on the calendar. That got us to the end of the year, anyway. If anyone asked me where we would be sleeping on any given night, I could have told them. That was yesterday. Now we sat stalled at the Mill Creek campground, I had a knot of anxiety lodged in my chest, and my heart was pumping hard up into my throat.

The past months had been so full—first of trauma and loss and then of planning, packing, and even excitement. Taking Norma along with us had seemed like such a good idea when we proposed it; it had felt almost too good, too easy, like we could live our lives the same way with just an additional, easy-to-take-care-of traveler. But the wind and the waiting had stopped all our forward motion, and now the ground had just sort of dropped out from under me. I sat down and took everything in.

My thoughts drifted toward the big picture. I have long felt that I was put on this earth to make a difference, and my work always reflected this: I have counseled children and teens, coordinated disaster relief efforts after a devastating flood, volunteered at the local juvenile justice center, raised funds for countless nonprofits, and participated in a movement to encourage fathers to become more involved in their children's lives. Waiting there in that damp campground, I could not help but let my fears surface.

Were we just driving around, I wondered, using up fossil fuels and taking Norma sightseeing? Had I lost the one thing that felt so essential to my identity in exchange for a full-time caregiving role that I felt in no way prepared for? Would depression fill the void of purpose in me as it had in the past?

How could I make a difference in this world by taking care of just this one person, this woman who had always been so independent and self-sufficient? With Norma along, I would not be able to serve the communities I had grown used to serving. Without a larger community to support—and to support me in return—would I still be able to make an impact? I had so many gifts to give the world, I thought, but not caregiving. That was not one of my gifts. It felt small, insignificant, and isolating to me.

I had felt this way once before, when I quit my job to live full-time on the road. It was only in the previous season in Baja California that our work with a small orphanage in a village there had been helping finally to fill that hole in my life. We had planned to go back to visit the orphanage the following winter, but Norma was not ready to travel across the southern border with us quite yet. I was selfishly afraid that I would not be fulfilled on this journey. It seemed like taking care of one person was keeping me from supporting so many others.

Tim and I had just taken this leap of faith, and already I was questioning my ability to gently float along. I knew I needed to let go, but, man, it was hard!

That afternoon Tim tried to reassure me. "You like photography," he said. "Maybe if you dive into taking photos it will take your mind off things for a while." But I was not yet willing to pull myself out of my own personal pity party.

Sure, I liked photography, but how would that fill my need to change the world, or even improve my small corner of it? How would that soothe my feelings of loneliness as I struggled to put my own needs to one side and now focus on Norma's?

I pulled out my MacBook Pro and typed up a few thoughts on the travel blog I had been keeping since the summer of 2011. Although maybe only a dozen or so people had followed my posts over the years, it felt like a community I could reach out to. Maybe these people would continue to be interested as my writing transitioned from the topics of nature and travel to assisted living on wheels. Perhaps by sharing this journey in writing as well as in photographs, I would not feel so alone.

I posted a blog entry entitled "Changes in Latitudes, Changes in Attitudes," inspired by some of my favorite Jimmy Buffett lyrics. Then Norma settled into a book while Tim and I slipped into our rain gear and took Ringo for a walk along the lakeshore, collecting a few beautifully tumbled rocks to show Norma, our resident "rock hound," when we got back. By the time we returned to the motor home, several people had commented on the blog post. We read the comments to Norma, hoping they would excite her as much as her snail-mail delivery once had.

"Who says you can't have an adventure in your nineties?" one comment read.

"Let it flow" was another. *"There are so many wonderful things to see and do that are totally unplanned. It's ALL-good. Spontaneity rules."*

Despite Norma's tired look, a glimmer of fascination crept into her eyes. "Those people care about our journey?" she mused. "I don't know why."

I was surprised to feel a wave of relief come over me as we shared these words and joined in Norma's delight in them. Tim was right, in a way. I did find some solace in taking photographs— but not in the photographs alone. The sense of community I felt through sharing our photos and stories is what gave me comfort. They showed me how hard I was clinging to my expectations.

There was no getting around it: the weather disrupted our travels plans, living with Norma disrupted the flow of our lives, and this new arrangement had certainly disrupted my sense of self. I was lonely, emotionally disheveled, and meeting the road, my husband, and my mother-in-law all over again. I had to flow with it instead of against it.

These blog commenters could see something I had been unable to discern through my fears: even perpetual nomads need to slow down and let go of expectations. Suddenly, all the plans we had made for the next four months were put into a different perspective. From then on our plan was a simple one: not to have one.

◊ ◊ ◊

We sat in windy Mackinaw City for three days before the authorities allowed large-profile vehicles to drive on the bridge. Making it across "Big Mac" was a rite of passage of sorts. It felt different in the Upper Peninsula—more rugged and remote, to be sure. An impenetrable birch, cedar, and pine forest dominated the landscape on the north side of the road, and the roadway itself was piped with a never-ending border of goldenrod, cattails, and Queen Anne's lace. On the south side, the vastness of Lake Michigan and its untouched shoreline gave hints of an undeveloped yesteryear.

Norma's gaze remained steady, looking out the large dining room window as we crossed into the central time zone.

I announced, "Welcome to Wisconsin!"

She excitedly raised her voice loud enough for me to hear in the front seat. "Oh, I've never been to Wisconsin." Neither Tim nor I had known that she had never crossed the border to Michigan's neighboring state. It had not taken long for us to reach uncharted territory.

"This is going to be fun!" Tim and I said to each other.

The Dairy State presented us with rolling hills dotted with red barns, hay bales, and black-and-white cows—scenes begging to be featured on a jigsaw puzzle. Many of the old barns had fading advertisements painted on them, like CHEW MAIL POUCH TOBACCO or DRINK COCA-COLA, and we could see Norma becoming a bit nostalgic as we passed them by. Norma wanted to see Mount Rushmore, and we were determined to get her there before her health declined further.

◊ ◊ ◊

When trying to get from point A to point B with no particular destination in between, many RVers try to dry camp somewhere without any utility hookups. Finding a place to park a traveling home for the night at no cost is easier than one might think. By using an amazing application on our iPad, Tim and I have been able to map out our sleeping spots ahead of time. Truck stops are an option, but the idling diesels can be quite noisy. Instead, we have found that big-box stores, Native American casinos, and Cracker Barrel restaurants can be quite accommodating to the RV community.

The rules are simple: always call ahead for permission, and never stay more than one night. Sometimes it has worked out beautifully, yielding views of rolling farm fields or vast plains. Sometimes, well, there has been a carnival or a monster truck rally happening in the parking lot that night. On these occasions, the smell of popcorn and cotton candy, or of exhaust fumes from a beefed-up truck rolling over a row of derelict cars, spilled into our trailer. But we soon became oblivious to the sounds of automobiles, the laughter of children, and the music from an old merry-go-round spinning around in a roped-off area of the lot. We were simply thankful to be safely off the road for the day, relaxing in our home, our feet kicked up, and enjoying whatever Tim had rustled up for dinner.

For many years we had counted on these types of places to stop, but we might have neglected to share with our parents just how often we slept in Walmart parking lots. This would be a preferred method of travel on this trip as well, so we needed to prepare Norma. Neither of us knew how she would react to simply pulling over and calling, say, a Home Depot "home sweet home" for the night.

We broke Norma into this type of camping at the Oneida Nation casino parking lot in Green Bay, Wisconsin, where we parked under some tall shade trees. It was one afternoon not much farther along in the trip when we pulled into our first Walmart parking lot in Blue Earth, Minnesota, intending to spend the night.

Norma impressed us with her willingness to leave her comfort zone and sleep in such places—we know many people who would not. We were testing the waters early on so we would know, going forward, what kind of sleeping arrangements we could count on and where she would draw the line.

The memory of those blog commenters telling us to loosen up was still fresh in my mind. I had started to feel like my role was within the top tiers of Maslow's hierarchy of needs, while Tim was taking care of the bottom layers. Tim focused on food, water, shelter, and safety, while I was more inclined to try to enrich our lives with a sense of connection, spontaneity, creativity, experience, and purpose. I did not want us to just expect the unexpected; I wanted us to embrace it completely.

We parked the motor home on the only level spot in the Walmart lot, and then took Norma out to explore our surroundings. For expediency, we wheeled her across the street with Ringo in tow and headed toward the local Dairy Queen, for there was something special behind it we wanted to show her.

"Behold," Tim said, delighting in the moment.

And there we stood, in front of the largest—and I believe only—Jolly Green Giant statue in the world. The frozen-vegetable icon loomed fifty-five feet above us.

I thought stopping at this silly statue early in the trip would set a tone for everything else that came after. It meant that we were up for anything. We hoped it might loosen us up, maybe even take some of the seriousness from Norma's face.

Clad in green herself—an embroidered sweater—Norma rose from her wheelchair and hobbled toward the statue. When she got there, she handed off her cane and put her hands on her hips to imitate the Giant's pose. I pulled out my camera and started taking photographs in between deep belly laughs, absolutely tickled at the sight of this tiny, normally reserved woman hamming it up with the Jolly Green Giant.

This was the first time in years that Tim or I had seen her smile—I mean, *really* smile. Sifting through boxes of old snapshots in her home over the five weeks we had spent preparing to leave on this adventure, both of us had been struck by the fact that we could not find one image with her smiling. "I just can't take a nice picture," she told me. "Never could." It was a matter of fact to her.

Already, just days into our adventure, she was showing us a side of her we had never seen—not just happy and smiling but silly too. She was simply enjoying herself. From the Jolly Green Giant's shadow, she made her way down the path to a plywood cutout of Little Green Sprout, his advertising sidekick. Norma nonchalantly poked her head through the rough-cut hole and posed for another photo; the look on her face was full of mischief and joy. I suddenly realized there was more life in this woman than I had ever imagined. She had a knack for embracing both the sublime and the absurd. She did not shy away from experience; instead she leaned into it with a wave or a funky pose and without questioning why.

Maybe she had always had this talent in her but it had never been given the opportunity to grow. Maybe age and illness offered her a permission slip to do things that would have embarrassed her younger self. Perhaps, unmoored from her Presque Isle home and all of its responsibilities, she felt freer to just be. Maybe she was done worrying about taking a "nice" picture and was ready to take "real" pictures instead: silly, sarcastic, joyful, and true.

In this moment my heart warmed. The woman I had known for approaching two decades, and Tim his whole life, was now not only "Norma" and "Mom"; she had become "Miss Norma." *This ninety-year-old woman isn't done,* I said to myself. It was then that I believed we were about to begin learning lessons from the most improbable of all people: my mother-in-law.

We continued on our way along Interstate 90 through the Heartland, completely giving ourselves over to the roadside attractions. We did not adjust our route to Mount Rushmore because we did not need to: I-90 was lined with goofy places worth stopping at. On previous trips, Tim and I had sometimes stopped at these places; other times we had gone right by them. Now we made a conscious effort to interrupt our drive whenever something tickled us. Norma's smile inspired us to keep her laughing.

To that end, the next obvious stop was Mitchell, South Dakota, home of the world's only Corn Palace—or, as the locals call it, the world's largest bird feeder. Historically, the palace was built to celebrate the abundance of the year's harvest. The edifice is sided with themed murals made entirely of corn, straw, and other natural materials, and it is redesigned every year. As luck would have it, we arrived during the Corn Palace Festival, the time of year when the latest design is unveiled. The streets were closed to traffic, and all things maize were being highlighted.

"You and Ringo stand over here," Tim told his mom as I took a photograph of them standing next to a giant anthropomorphic corncob. Only a short time into our trip, we could see that Norma was really warming up to Ringo and that they were becoming fast pals.

As we traveled the next 275 miles from Mitchell to Rapid City, a few things stood out in the South Dakota landscape: massive fields of cultivated sunflowers, a tremendous lack of trees, and an abundance of billboards. After being teased by hundreds of hand-painted signs, we just had to go to Wall Drug.

It was ninety-eight degrees outside, so this sprawling, air-conditioned tourist attraction of international renown was an obvious stop for us. The original proprietor had lured motorists into his business, established in 1931, by offering free ice water to parched travelers heading west to see the nearby national monument. We each enjoyed a glass ourselves.

As we made our way through the maze of merchandise to find postcards to send back home, Norma stopped to pet a stuffed bison, its massive stature dwarfing her own. She also did not hesitate to climb aboard a larger-than-life jackalope statue that she spied in an outdoor courtyard between the buildings. She was coming alive before our very eyes.

After setting up in a campground outside Rapid City, South Dakota, we arrived the following day at our first big destination: Mount Rushmore National Memorial, located in the Black Hills in Keystone. It had been conceived in 1923 to promote tourism in the state, and then Gutzon Borglum and four hundred workers spent fourteen years sculpting the colossal sixty-foot-high carvings of U.S. presidents George Washington, Thomas Jefferson, Theodore Roosevelt, and Abraham Lincoln out of the native granite formation. We soon realized that their heads were just about the same height as the entire Jolly Green Giant statue.

While in the park's visitor center, my shy mother-in-law joyfully pressed down a plunger of a mock blasting detonator at an interactive display, laughing hysterically when a film clip of a real explosion on the mountain appeared on a screen in front of her. A nine-year-old boy cracked up as he watched, taken by Norma's youthful antics. Soon his family followed suit and everyone around us was suddenly filled with joy as they encouraged Norma to blow up some more stuff.

We started recognizing that Norma's joy was infectious—not just for us but for others too. There was the part of her that needed caregiving and required the kind of vigilant support that had inspired such fear in me our first morning on the road. But we were discovering another side to Norma as well. This Norma,

Miss Norma, gave us something priceless in return for our care: her pure delight, her adventurous spirit, her willingness to play with the world, to touch and taste with eager abandon.

We did not know if her interest in those huge presidential sculptures was because of her interest in American history, geology, or art, or simply because it had been an amazing feat. It did not matter. She could not take her eyes off the giant stone busts, and she read every interpretive sign in the park. Norma was a sponge, soaking up every drop she could. And soon enough, so were we.

◊ ◊ ◊

Norma could not find the words to create a bucket list, although at first that is what we were hoping for. If for no other reason, it would have helped with planning. "Oh, I don't know" she would say over and over again, and it became clear very early in our preparations that we were not going to get a list out of her.

Sometimes I felt frustrated that she would not participate much in the planning. Was it her age? I wondered. Was her brain unable to retrieve language easily? Was she simply not used to dreaming or being asked her opinion about things? But I soon grew to appreciate the opportunities her reticence to make a list gave us.

Without one, we could really go with the flow. There was so much to see and do, and more than anything, Norma just wanted to enjoy life. A bucket list would be much too limiting. This trip was not about checking off predetermined items. As we had quickly learned from those first delayed plans at the Mackinac Bridge and our experiences at roadside attractions, this trip was instead about living in the present moment, embracing whatever came our way. There would be no regrets and no need to race against time.

Sitting here at our campground, we decided that we needed to come up with some kind of plan, though—some way to decide where to go next. Fortunately, we had a few hints. Norma loved geology. She was patriotic. Although she had never been a professional artist, she had studied art in college, and I believed art and creation were at the core of her being. Over the years, she had woven baskets that she then donated to raise money for charity. She had made silver jewelry too, as well as thrown clay pots and sketched in charcoal. And her stunning garden hinted at an interest in the natural world.

Simply saying "Yes" when opportunities arose would allow Norma's interests to inform our route. We were committed to a wakeful trust and collaboration with what was showing up for us. No experience was too insignificant for us to be present for. The difference between being "alive" and "living" was really not so subtle, after all. Norma was already showing us that. We noticed that all of us were becoming more radiant, more fully alive, and more willing to continue saying "Yes." We sought opportunities to put ourselves out there, hoping to encounter something new, fun, or touching.

So I was not too surprised when Tanya, a friend I had not heard from in fifteen years, emailed me out of the blue, saying, "I've been thinking about you, I hope you are doing well. We now live in South Dakota. Write when you get a chance."

"We happen to be in South Dakota right now!" I quickly wrote back, tickled by the synchronicity. I said that we were traveling with Tim's mom, and I sent her the link to Norma's Facebook page explaining that it was easier to chronicle our adventures there than writing about them in my blog.

"Does your mother-in-law like beer?" Tanya oddly replied. She went on: "Josh and I now own a brewery in Spearfish, and I would love to bring some of our craft beer by the campground for Miss Norma to try."

Without hesitation, I replied, "Yes!"

My long-lost friend soon arrived with three six-packs of Crow Peak Brewery's finest. Tim cracked open a can of its award-winning Canyon Cream Ale, poured it into a glass, and handed it to his mom. Norma took a refreshing gulp, looked up with a twinkle in her eye, and said, "I don't think I could do *this* in the nursing home!" Then she raised her cold beer again and took a second gulp.

The profound meaning of this utterance reverberated in my body. Here, at last, was purpose: to give a dying woman, who had so loved and nurtured others throughout her long life, the gift of discovery and delight in her final days.

Everything shifted. None of us knew what was coming next. But one thing we now knew was this: taking Norma on the road was already turning out to be a good decision.

CHAPTER 4

Trust

YELLOWSTONE NATIONAL PARK, WYOMING

SEPTEMBER

[Tim]

The Bighorn Mountains stretch across northern Wyoming and southern Montana, with many cirques, U-shaped valleys, and glacial lakes between the peaks that can reach more than 13,000 feet into the air, and they were the first bit of elevation we encountered on the trip. "We can do this," I said just before our gas-powered motor home began climbing the winding, single-lane road up the side of one of these mountains. "People do this in RVs all the time." I could feel the sweat from my palms dampening the steering wheel.

During such anxious moments, Ramie would get very quiet and rarely use her fair share of oxygen. I chalked it up this time to her overreacting, knowing she would calm after we crested the hill. Then, as we approached the top, something felt terribly wrong. I had the gas pedal pressed all the way to the floor but the motor home barely continued lurching forward. A hot September sun was blazing on me from the south through the side window, adding to my already elevated level of discomfort. As our speed dropped from forty to thirty to twenty to ten miles per hour, I glanced for places to pull over. There were none—just a steep, thousand-foot drop. I know now that pushing the TOW/HAUL knob on the end of the windshield wiper lever would have prevented this situation, but at the time I was still new to driving the rig, so it was just us, our rapidly dwindling power, and nowhere to go but up.

"Are we going to make it?" Ramie asked, biting down on her knuckles.

"Sure we will," I bluffed. I knew that if we stopped in the middle of the road now, we would be in a world of trouble.

Mom sat in her seat at the dining table, peering out the window at the incredible scenery, oblivious to our dilemma. She either trusted that we would make it or, more than likely, could not hear our somewhat panicked exchange.

My foot was about ready to go through the floorboard when I spied a sign indicating that we were approaching the top of the pass. "Just a little bit more, please," I implored under my breath. Just when we were almost at a complete stop, the road pitched downward toward the next valley. Like on a seesaw, we had reached the tipping point.

"I knew we would make it, honey," I said with as much confidence as I could summon. The road to that day's destination was truly all downhill from here.

Ramie was just beginning to breathe again when we eventually rolled into the tiny town of Ten Sleep, Wyoming. "Why do you suppose this place is called Ten Sleep?" we all blurted out after passing the sign welcoming us to this community of 257 residents. We later learned that the ranching town, rich in history, had been named such because it was ten days' travel, or ten "sleeps," between major Sioux camps there at the time.

Old wooden wagons overflowing with blooming flowers greeted us at the entrance of the funky campground/horse motel located at the west end of town. The owner was an accommodating fellow who clearly took pride in his place and was busy planting trees when we drove in. It felt like an oasis after traversing the barren heights of the Bighorns. He greeted us at the office, checked us in, offered us bottles of ice-cold water, and then went with us to our site to make sure we all would be comfortable for the night. We collectively took our first deep breath of the very long day after we leveled the motor home and hooked up the utilities.

Our camp was across a dirt road from the local rodeo grounds, and the high school football field was in sight as well. We could see that the players had just finished practice and were milling around the rodeo stands, waiting for their rides home. Mom noticed there were a couple of girls in the group, all suited up with shoulder pads and carrying their helmets.

"Aren't those girls in those uniforms?" Mom asked. We had to agree that they were. There are not enough boys in Ten Sleep to field a team, we later learned, so the girls are welcome to play too. "Well, that's neat to see," she added.

I glanced at Ramie and we smiled at each other.

◊ ◊ ◊

One hundred fifty miles and not ten but one sleep later, we proudly flashed my mom's National Parks Senior Pass as we rolled through the narrow entryway of Yellowstone National Park's east gate with only an inch to spare on each side of our mirrors. "Welcome to Yellowstone, Norma," Ramie yelled to the back of the motor home. She shouted such greetings to Mom every time we crossed a state line; it seemed appropriate to start announcing national parks too.

Our country's first national park, Yellowstone is a nearly 3,500-square-mile wilderness that rests on top of a volcanic hot spot. It features dramatic canyons, forests, alpine rivers, hot springs, and gushing geysers, including its most famous, Old Faithful. It is also home to hundreds of animal species, including bears, wolves, elk, antelope, otters, and bison.

"Oh, I hope that we see a bear," Mom said as we drove into the park.

"Well, I'm pretty sure we will see some wildlife!" Ramie replied. The words were barely out of her mouth before I was quickly stepping on the brakes to join the rest of the motoring tourists halted ahead of us: a herd of bison was crossing the road. Ramie quickly pulled out her camera to capture Mom's surprised reaction to a huge male bison that was looking into her window; his grunts filled the air with stale breath before he eventually strolled across the road nonplussed. Ringo was not impressed by the spectacle he was also witnessing through a window. A growl under his breath let Mom know he was on duty, ready to protect her.

As Ramie worked at taking the perfect shot, she continued: "We will definitely see some bubbling mud pits and geysers while we are here too. This place is amazing, Norma!"

We held true to that promise when we arrived at the Upper Geyser Basin a few days later. "This is the largest concentration of geysers in the world, Mom," I said as we stood in the parking lot, gazing at the sight. Hundreds of steam plumes were rising in the distance. The two-square-mile basin contained nearly one-quarter of the earth's geysers. Besides spouting geysers, there were also colorful hot springs and steaming fumaroles, which emitted sulfurous gases. The smell of rotten eggs was already wafting toward us.

"And we can wheel you in your chair to see a lot of them," Ramie added.

"Really? How can we possibly do that?" Mom asked from her wheelchair, slightly baffled.

We explained that not only did this basin contain many unique geological features, but also the National Park Service had built a wheelchair-friendly boardwalk around most of them.

"I guess that will work," she finally said, sounding only slightly apprehensive.

This was our first big stop after visiting Mount Rushmore. I had pushed her in her wheelchair during that visit, but all the trails there were paved, had guardrails, and looked relatively safe. Here the boardwalk was made of wood and stood only a few inches above the fragile crust covering this volcanic area. There was no guardrail, simply a two-by-four-inch board forming a low barrier. The only thing that would keep Mom from the hissing rocks and bubbling mud was me, and I was not too sure she really trusted me with her safety on this proposed adventure.

Old Faithful was just a short stroll away from where we stood. Ramie and I had seen it erupt many times over the past thirty years, but at the age of ninety, Mom was seeing it for the first time. We watched her face in anticipation of her awe and wonder as nearly eight thousand gallons of boiling water shot at least a hundred feet into the air in a spectacle that took several minutes. When the waters calmed, the international audience clapped its hands in appreciation of Mother Nature's show. Mom could only stare with her mouth wide open, apparently overcome by the splendor.

As the crowd dispersed, we took to the boardwalks, passing geologic features with names like Anemone, Beehive, Lion, Spasmodic, Beauty, and Chromatic. I pushed Mom as close to the edge as I could so that she could witness them in all their magnificence. We waited patiently for the ground to rumble and for the short surges that sent water and steam high into the air.

"Don't get us too close," she shouted as drops of geyser water fell upon us.

We had walked for a few miles when Mom decided to give me a break. She asked to walk behind her wheelchair the last hundred yards up the boardwalk to the Morning Glory Pool, a brilliant-green hot spring laced with orange and yellow edges. Once there, she studied it for a long time. The colors created by the heat-sensitive bacteria that existed in the extreme temperatures were mesmerizing, and it seemed she could not take her eyes off the pool.

This pool marked the end of the wheelchair-accessible trail. Farther along was a gravel path that led to Biscuit Basin and a slew of other geysers. I was excited by Mom's willingness to go this far, and I asked her if she would like us to continue by rolling her off the boardwalk and going onward.

"Sure I do," she shot back without hesitation.

The uneven trail was an easy push for a while, but the slope increased and I was soon running out of energy. We were nearly halfway up the hill, and she wanted to press on, fully enraptured by the experience. Despite her insistence that she could walk the rest of the way to the top, the question now was whether I would be able to get her down, not up.

"I think we should turn back," I told her.

Using the wheelchair's hand brakes and with measured steps, we returned to the relatively flat but rocky trail at the base of the incline. Still amped from endorphins and adrenaline, I spotted an informal trail that led to a hot spring we could see steaming at the edge of a fast-moving stream. I thought I would try to get Mom down to see it.

As I pushed and pulled her chair along the dirt path, hitting roots and rocks, her tiny body bobbed back and forth like a rag doll. Her wrinkled hands clung tightly to the wheelchair's armrests, her brows furrowed, and her lips pressed into a small, tense line. She looked uncomfortable and was perhaps a bit frightened, her body taut and resistant against the present situation.

We had come all this way. But although we could now say we had triumphantly crested the Bighorn Mountains, we were still on rocky terrain emotionally. There were years of distance between us, yet to be bridged. In the past few weeks, I had come to know the silly and adventurous side of my mom and I wanted to show her everything I had seen, no limits. Could she trust me enough to let me take her off the beaten path, to navigate her final days?

◊ ◊ ◊

I was a little more than three months old when I first learned about trust. I had just met my new parents. It was nine days before Christmas in 1957 and they had just received an early holiday gift: me.

Dad and Mom both grew up during the country's Great Depression. My mom's father was sporadically employed in Toledo, Ohio, and could not provide much for his family. "We would share five thin slices of fried bologna between the six of us for dinner," Mom would often tell my sister and me while we were growing up. My dad's family lived in Toledo and was not much better off. He was sent to an aunt's farm every summer to work and to take some of the financial pressure off his single mom. At least he found there was more food on the table while he lived out in the country.

They both volunteered to serve in World War II. Dad was a clerk in the Army Air Corps, a precursor of the air force, and was stationed at Hickam Field in Hawaii. Mom followed her older brother, Ralph, into the navy. Ralph was seventeen and underage when he enlisted, but my grandfather would not let my mom enlist until she turned twenty. When she was old enough she joined the WAVES (Women Accepted for Voluntary Emergency Services). After basic training in New York, she rode a cold train across Canada, south to New Mexico, and then west to California and the San Diego Naval Hospital, where she served as a nurse for a year and a half. She liked to tell everyone that she had briefly qualified for international pay because the troop train had left U.S. soil. "Every little bit helps," she would say. It seemed she had not been admiring those young female football players in the town of Ten Sleep from a place of distance; I think her belief in "girl power" was as strong as when she joined the ranks of the first women in the navy, nearly seventy years before.

Mom's brother, Ralph, and my dad became good buddies after the war. They had both moved back to Toledo and would get together to have a beer or work on cars. He introduced my mom and dad to each other at a bar one night, and they got married soon after. Later, when they were beaming with the national optimism that prevailed in the United States during the 1950s, my parents found out they could not conceive children. After fostering several children for Catholic Charities during that decade, the organization finally gave them one they could call their own.

When I was about six years old, my parents told me I was adopted. I was just old enough then to understand the concept, though it really did not make a difference to me if I was biological or not. They were the only parents I had ever known.

That was just before we got a call that a baby sister was coming. Mom and Dad had applied for another child right after my adoption, and it had taken that long for the paperwork to come through. I remember hearing our beige rotary telephone ring. Mom asked me to answer it. I quickly handed over the clunky handset when the caller asked to speak to her. She became so excited during the conversation that I could not wait for her to hang up and tell me what was going on. "Your baby sister arrives next week!" she exclaimed, more animated than I had ever seen her. And here I did not even know that we were expecting one.

The day Stacy arrived was a happy one for all of us. When I got off the school bus, I ran down the sidewalk to our modest split-level home on Middlebury Street and raced up the stairs until I reached the first door on the left. There, in the corner of the bedroom near the window, I caught a first glimpse of my sister in her crib. She was small and pink, and had very little hair on her head.

Mom was a homemaker; she cooked the meals, made my Halloween costumes, and tutored me with flash cards. Dad worked a decent job with the regional utility company. We were solidly middle class—quite an accomplishment for a man who had lost his father at age two and who had only a high school education.

My dad's job was white collar, but he had to work swing shifts and holidays. Day shifts would roll into night shifts that would roll into afternoon shifts with no apparent rhyme or reason.

Some days I would catch only a glimpse of him as he was getting up or going to bed. I would sometimes listen at the bedroom door as the noise from the electric fan masked his snores. I often longed for him to be able to come outside and play baseball or build a birdhouse with me.

Perhaps because of this, I bonded with my mom more than with my dad. After all, she had nothing but time at home to spend with me. Armed with a copy of Dr. Benjamin Spock's *Common Sense Book of Baby and Child Care,* she heeded the doctor's words to trust her instincts and be confident in her parenting skills. She applied many of Dr. Spock's principles to my upbringing: routines are nice, but babies do not need a strict regimen; do not fret if your baby acts funny; ideas about good parenting should evolve; babies need love.

By no means did this approach to child-rearing turn me into a narcissistic child lacking respect for his parents, as some of Dr. Spock's critics asserted would happen. Quite the opposite, I would say. But looking back at it now, I can see that this was probably where I got my fiercely independent streak. My mom trusted herself to raise me right and trusted that I would become a good person because of her efforts. And her confidence helped me learn that I could trust myself. My biggest hope now was that I would not disappoint her.

I can see how this same philosophy may have shaped my mom too. When Dr. Spock's book came out in 1946, physicians in the United States had already established themselves as the voices of authority in medical matters. Spock gave postwar parents permission to be confident in their decisions. My mom must have reached for some of this confidence when she made the decision to refuse cancer treatment and told the doctors that she was *"hitting the road."*

I was now a grown man. Mom and I for many years had been separated by time and distance, and we had no biological bond. My dad and my sister were dead. My mom now relied on me to feed her, to make her medical and financial decisions, and to keep her safe. Could Mom, in her time of old age, fragility, and illness, count on me to have her best interests at heart on this journey? Did she trust me as I trusted her?

I had forgone having a family of my own because I did not want this kind of responsibility. The thought of going to bed each night with a house full of people depending on me to get up the next morning and provide all the financial and emotional security a parent should give was so daunting. Mom's present situation was forcing me to revisit this commitment. Our roles now reversed, she had to trust me with what was left of her life.

◊ ◊ ◊

I tipped the wheelchair back as we continued making our way toward the hot spring next to the river, guiding the big rear wheels backward over a giant tree root. My mom, still clenching the armrests with her hands, face tightly knit, held all her muscles in a defensive state, as if preparing for disaster.

"Norma," Ramie said. "Tim's got you. It's okay. You can let go."

I felt a sort of pause, a tipping point, like the one we had felt coming over the mountain. We could not go on resisting each other. We had spent so much time growing independently, but now we were interdependent. We had to learn to be.

And then something glorious happened: Mom let everything go. She spread her arms wide, as if she were hugging the world. The corners of her mouth lifted, her chest opened, and an expression of pure joy came onto her face. Her jubilance was in-fectious, spreading to me as well as Ramie, who quickly snapped a photograph and captured the moment for posterity.

The true magic of Yellowstone that day took place not within the main attractions, but during that bumpy trip down to the stream. For so long my mom had been the strong and self-less woman who had experienced most of life's difficulties—economic hardship, war, infertility, the deaths of a child and her husband—and who was more comfortable saying "Don't bother, don't worry about me" than she was asking for help. But now she needed me—she needed us. If Ramie and I were to truly care for her, we all needed to trust one another; we all had to allow ourselves to be vulnerable to the journey, these places, each other.

In those arms thrown wide, Mom was unfolding her whole being with complete trust. In that moment we all understood that it was through trust that we experience a most profound source of freedom. Without trust, we imprison our joy and can find ourselves literally holding our breath. But if we take only a moment to remember that someone else is there to support us, we find the freedom to let go, ask "Why not?," and enjoy every bump in the road.

Later, as we followed a flat section of the paved trail that led back to the visitor center, Mom surprised us again. "You've pushed me all day," she said to me. "Let me give you a break; let me push for a while."

No one had ever pushed me in a wheelchair before, let alone my elderly mom. The people who came upon us on the trails must have thought she had pushed me for some distance, judg-ing by the sidelong glances and shaking heads we encountered. In fact it was not for very long at all, and Ramie took a short video of the effort, which we replay whenever we want a good laugh. The hikers we passed could not possibly have known that what we experienced that day was so much more than a ride in a wheelchair; we felt the mountain's and each other's strong embrace, and tasted the sweet freedom of both letting go and being held after so much exertion.

Ramie and I continued to remind Mom of that day whenever we saw she might not trust my wheelchair agility or any other aspect of our journey. "Timmy has you, Norma," Ramie would say. "Remember our trip to Yellowstone?"

CHAPTER 5

Perspective

BOULDER, COLORADO

SEPTEMBER

[Tim]

From Yellowstone National Park in Wyoming, we drove the motor home south along the shadow of the Wind River Range, passing through the Great Divide Basin and then skirting the Medicine Bow Mountains on our way into Colorado. Fall was in full swing and the aspen leaves were quaking, their stunning gold color contrasting remarkably with the cobalt-blue sky that can be found only in the American West.

We had been living at elevation for over a month by now. Ramie and I were relieved that Mom was not experiencing many of the physical problems people have when they first get to higher altitudes. In fact, she was considerably mobile when we arrived at our new spot in the foothills below Rocky Mountain National Park. She was able to get around with confidence by walking behind her lightweight wheelchair. If she got tired, she could sit down on the seat to catch her breath before moving on. Each day here Mom would ease herself down the motor-home steps and go for a walk around some of the campground loops, returning to our campsite on the Big Thompson River with obvious satisfaction. Sitting in her wheelchair poised at the rushing river's edge and with Ringo by her side, she would spend the days sipping tea, knitting, reading books, or working on sudoku puzzles. Life was good for her, we thought.

But when we left Michigan the month before, both Ramie and I had noticed that my mom's left foot and ankle were swollen. With Dad's death and her cancer diagnosis coming so soon after, we really had not had time to give that observation much thought. Now we saw that the swelling had moved up her leg all the way to the knee.

Her swollen leg was not the only thing that had started to concern us. We also noticed she would often get extremely dizzy when she got up to go to the bathroom at the other end of the motor home. Her nose ran constantly, and she fell in and out of sleep all day long. Mom was also reminded of her cancer diagnosis every time she used the bathroom. Although she had no pain or any indication that there was a tumor growing inside her, she bled through a couple of sanitary pads every day, and she hated it.

"This is not good," I said. "Perhaps the elevation is having an effect on her circulation after all."

"I wonder if the problem is the side effects of some of her prescription medications," Ramie replied.

Mom *was* taking quite a few medications. We went on the Internet to look for some answers.

Mom took opioids three times a day to alleviate her chronic arthritis pain. We found that opioids likely cause drowsiness, mental confusion, nausea, constipation, and, depending on the dosage, can depress respiration. Mom was exhibiting many of these symptoms and yet was still suffering from pain. Another drug, for high cholesterol—prescribed by a doctor who had left town many years earlier and therefore Mom had never followed up with him—might explain her runny nose. Recent appointments had shown that Mom's cholesterol level was not even high anymore.

Our research also revealed considerable evidence about marijuana and its derivatives that was promising. We learned that cannabidiol (CBD) and tetrahydrocannabinol (THC)—the two main components in marijuana—both belong to a unique class of compounds known as cannabinoids. THC is best known as the psychoactive ingredient in marijuana that can alter mood, behavior, and perception. This component is also the one that heightens senses, makes a person feel relaxed, and sometimes prompts food cravings, better known as the "munchies." Although that might have been really good for Mom—she could stand to gain a little weight—I knew she would not be interested in any of that.

CBD, however, is nonpsychoactive and is currently being studied for its significant medical benefits. Ramie and I read about research that showed it had positive effects on patients seeking relief from inflammation, pain, anxiety, psychosis, seizures, and spasms. We also discovered that in clinical studies CBD had reduced the size of certain cancer tumors.

We felt a responsibility to make sure Mom was as comfortable and pain-free as possible. But if the side effects of her medications were inhibiting her from having the confidence or energy to fully embrace life, then we wanted to explore other options.

CBD was worth a try. After all, here we were in Colorado, which in 2014 had become one of only four states in the country where marijuana was currently legal and accessible to any adult, even without a medical marijuana card. But we also knew that at some point we would have to actually talk to my mom about all of this.

Mom was starting to be particularly bothered by her swollen leg. Before leaving Presque Isle, she had made it clear to us that not only was she choosing to forgo cancer treatment, but she was done with doctors altogether. "No more poking or prodding," she had said. She wanted her privacy and her dignity. But we could tell she was uncomfortable. I asked Ramie if she would talk to her about using a cannabis cream, since I thought Mom might take it more seriously if she heard it from Ramie instead of me.

I had good reason to be hesitant. Once, when I was in high school—and my mom still did my laundry—I forgot to remove a marijuana joint from the breast pocket of my well-worn Levi's jean jacket before putting it in the clothes bin. There was never any conversation about it; that was just not my mom's way. But later I found a handwritten note in the pocket of my freshly laundered garment that stated:

I wish you would quit smoking this stuff.

—*Mom*

The joint had been neatly tucked in with the note, graciously spared from the wash, rinse, and spin cycles by the woman who so disliked the habit.

I stepped out of the motor home, nervously lingering near the screen door to overhear the conversation. Ramie asked Mom if she had ever heard of cannabis cream, a skin lotion that contained CBD and other essential oils, such as arnica, peppermint, and juniper. I was surprised to hear her say, "Oh sure."

"Would you be willing to try it?" Ramie boldly asked. "It is supposed to be good for pain and it might help your leg. We can get it here in Colorado."

"Sure. I suppose that might be good," she replied, barely giving it a second thought.

◊ ◊ ◊

My parents had never used recreational drugs, but pharmaceutical drugs had played an important role in keeping my dad alive.

In 1978, he suffered a heart attack, which required coronary bypass surgery. The first successful bypass operation on a human had occurred only ten years before, and even though by 1977 cardiac surgeons were performing one hundred thousand of these procedures a year, I was still worried about Dad's chances. I had just moved to Colorado from Ohio, and I remember flying back home to be with the family for the operation. (I later learned that Ramie's father died of a heart attack that same year.)

Fortunately, my dad survived the surgery, but it turned out that what Dad really had was coronary heart disease, a progressive illness. Nothing can truly cure it. He underwent two more surgeries after that first one. For nearly forty years he did everything his doctors instructed him to do, taking all the many prescribed medicines he was told would keep him alive, never questioning any of it.

When I first took Ramie to meet Dad, he was seventy-two years old and in fair shape, but he could not do as much as he probably wished he could. I saw him get frustrated by his physical limitations, which I am sure were mostly caused by having such a damaged heart. Over the years, though, I watched this frustration intensify as another household task or hobby became inaccessible to him. "Whatever you do, Son, don't get old," he would tell me. In the end, he could not heed his own advice.

On our annual summer visit the year before Dad died, Ramie and I entered their modest brick house to find a man who was totally disheveled and out of sorts. "Thank God you got here when you did," Mom exclaimed when she saw us coming through the back door. Mom, beside herself, told us they had been homebound for weeks because he could not operate the family car; Dad had run their grey Jeep Liberty off the road the last time he had tried to drive them the twenty miles to town for groceries and medicine.

In the living room, my dad sat on the edge of his favorite recliner. He was groggy and barely able to speak. It was already late in the afternoon, but his normally well-kept appearance was replaced with wild hair and a three days' growth of whiskers. Instead of his usual L.L.Bean slacks and a nice button-down, he wore baggy sweatpants and a dirty sweatshirt, with his undershirt sticking out. We both thought it was some kind of joke at first. Dad loved a good practical joke. But this, it turned out, was not one of them.

We could not get much from either Mom or Dad, except that his health had been deemed fine by all the doctors he had recently visited. Something was obviously wrong, though, and we decided we needed to get a handle on his medical situation.

"How can Dad possibly keep track of all these pills?" I asked, viewing the array of amber-colored plastic bottles on the kitchen cabinet shelf near the double sink.

"Timmy," Ramie said, "we have more bottles over here in this hutch."

"Is he really taking all of these?" we both wondered aloud.

We spread an armful of collected vials out on the living room floor in front of Dad's chair. The labels had long, unpronounceable names printed neatly below his name, with refills available many times over. We methodically went through each prescription, doing our best to get the names right, and held them up for Dad to see.

"What is this one for?" we asked with each one.

"Hell, I don't know," he said again and again, growing increasingly agitated.

My parents did not have the Internet available at their rural house, so we drove to the village library to do some research. We found Dad had the usual drugs to help reduce his blood pressure and cholesterol. One was for blood clots too. A diuretic helped him eliminate water during the day, and another pill stopped him from urinating at night. He needed one more to sleep. We learned that one of the medications made him nauseated, so he had gone to another doctor to get another pill for that. It went on and on. When we found that one medication was for depression, I broke down.

"Dad was a happy man all his life. What could possibly make him feel depressed?" I demanded.

It slowly dawned on me that the orderly, competent man I had known and loved was turning into the unkempt, confused, and unhappy person we had just left back at my parents' house—not because he was sick but because of an unchecked buildup of all the pharmaceuticals he was taking, which were meant to keep him healthy. At what point had his medical care crossed the threshold from managing illness to causing it?

If the individual side effects of these drugs were not troubling enough, we quickly found that the consequences of taking some of them together were even more frightening. There were twenty-four different medicine bottles in front of us and seemingly endless possibilities for cross-reactions. We tried to work backward and match his symptoms to each drug's acknowledged side effects. After closely examining information from the pharmaceutical companies, our findings began to explain a lot about his present condition.

Our next step was to make appointments with all the doctors who were prescribing to him. One by one we went with Dad to talk to each of them.

A pulmonary specialist fumbled with the referral papers sent to him by another doctor, his unease palpable as he struggled to answer even simple questions about my dad's health. It turned out he really did not know what he was treating my dad for; he had simply accepted the referral of another doctor. We canceled Dad's next appointment with him.

Another physician had no idea my dad was already taking a pill that would react with what he was prescribing. We filled him in on the research we had found, and he made the necessary adjustments.

Yet another doctor admitted that Dad's sleeping pill was probably too strong for him and agreed with us that an over-the-counter sleep aid would probably work just as well. It did.

We were late in the game, but it did not take long to see that a vocal and well-informed advocate was needed when dealing with the medical community. Medicare and a good prescription drug plan opened all sorts of doors for an elderly person like Dad, but no one was navigating him through the maze of this massive medical industry. Each doctor appeared to have a pill to cure any ailment, and Dad appeared to be taking all of them. Insurance companies were willing to pay the pharmaceutical companies, diagnoses were apparently easy to come by, and not one of the many specialists treating Dad's different ailments was talking to the others. Medicine had saved and prolonged my dad's life many times, but now those remedies were not working. At eighty-seven years of age, he was taking medications to ease the side effects of other medications, which added their own side effects and interactions. Was this living? Was this health?

We threw ourselves into the role of medical advocate, working to bring each doctor's recommendations together and eliminating some of the drugs Dad had been taking while also reducing the dosage of others. We stayed longer than usual that summer, making sure things were running smoothly before we left.

By the morning our Airstream left their driveway, my dad had returned to his normal, fully functioning self. Mom was out in her garden, pulling weeds and cutting lavender to dry for decorations. Dad was lying under his lawn tractor, fixing the mower belt. And Ramie and I were filled with emotions, grateful there would still be some quality left in my parents' lives. We were also much more educated about how modern medicine functions.

◊ ◊ ◊

Two days after Mom and Ramie talked about getting the cannabis-based skin cream, we all piled into the Wrangler and drove to a dispensary that I had previously visited. Mom sat in the backseat as we followed the two-lane road along the foothills to Boulder, unaware of our mission. The plains stretched out to the east of us, and we could see for miles on that clear day.

Almost prophetically, the Jeep's XM Satellite Radio was tuned to the all-reggae channel the Joint, Rasta music an appropriate soundtrack for a trek I had never thought I would be making with my mom.

This exploration seemed worth the awkwardness; in fact, we felt we had a responsibility to Mom to do this. We knew from my dad that there were times when traditional medicine healed, and times when it hurt more than it helped.

My mom was dying. She had chosen adventure and dignity for herself instead of invasive treatments that might prolong, or might just as easily shorten, her life. With those treatments, her last days most certainly would have been spent in hospitals, being pumped with toxic chemicals meant to kill her cancer. It seemed absurd, then, that she should spend the rest of her life half asleep from pain medications, joints so swollen that they prohibited mobility, and constantly bleeding. Quality of life was what Mom wanted. It was our job to explore all the options, even if that meant I had to bring up an uncomfortable topic with her.

"Tim, you have to tell your mom where we are going," Ramie insisted.

"You tell her," I nervously quipped back.

Ramie rarely pulled this card, but this time it just came out: "She's your mom. You have to tell her."

She was right—we could not just push Mom through the doors of a "pot shop" without fair warning.

Turning down the music and turning up the volume of my voice so she could hear in the back, I said, "Mom, we're going to a marijuana shop in Boulder to get you something for your pain. Okay?"

A strong voice emerged over the faint reggae rhythms: "Oh no we're not," she said.

Ramie whispered, "Semantics, Tim, semantics. She is okay with 'cannabis,' not 'marijuana.'"

She raised her voice and said, "Norma, remember when we talked the other day about the cannabis cream for your leg?"

"Yes, sure," she replied.

Ramie reassured her, saying, "That's where we're going, to see if we can get some of that cream for you."

"Oh, I guess that would be okay," she conceded.

"Phew. We are still on track," Ramie and I both said as the Jeep made its way through Boulder traffic.

Twenty minutes later I pulled into the dispensary's lot and parked in the handicap spot near the back door. During my college days in Boulder, this place had been an old Dunkin' Donuts shop. Instead of glazed donuts, pastries, and hot coffee, the storefront now offered cannabis flowers, edibles, and extracts. We got Mom into her wheelchair and rolled up to the security guard standing in the doorway.

"I am going to have to see if this young lady is old enough to enter," he joked, his modest physique making him look much less threatening than a bar bouncer. He scanned our IDs through a card reader. "I can assure you that your information will be private and will not be shared with the authorities," he added.

We entered, took a number from a kiosk, and sat in the crowded waiting room for our turn to go into the sales area in the back.

"Are you okay with this, Norma?" Ramie asked, surveying the diverse group we had joined in what looked and felt more like a lounge than anything else. We wanted her to be comfortable every step of the way.

It was late in the afternoon, and we seemed to have arrived with the after-work crowd. A nurse in scrubs sat in the corner, texting on her iPhone. Two house painters, their white T-shirts marred by colorful strokes of latex, sat across from us, and two guys with a local contractor's logo on their shirts were nearby talking about a job. A young white woman with dreadlocks and a nose ring paced around the front of the room, the smell of patchouli wafting off her. She eyed a digital numeric counter like the kind you might see at your local delicatessen, waiting for her number to come up. A businessman in a suit read a newspaper. I was struck by the normalcy and mix of the people in the room; here were regular people you might see at the grocery store or on the street. Mom must have agreed, replying "Yes" to Ramie's concern, her features appearing at ease.

When number forty-three was called, Ramie and I stood up. I handed the paper ticket to a woman who ushered the three of us through a sturdy door that opened into the dispensary's inner sanctum. The large, well-lit room was lined on three sides with glass display counters, and we were surprised to see the room packed with people, who were being attended to by about a dozen employees.

"I can help you over here," said a voice from the corner. We were motioned with the wave of a hand and we wheeled Mom across the busy room.

Our "budtender"—a playful take on "bartender"—was a pleasant young woman who managed her own section of the counter. Next to her was a glass-fronted refrigerator displaying the many marijuana edibles available. The assortment of cookies, brownies, cheesecakes, and candies, all labeled for potency, captivated Mom.

Besides the glass pipes, vaporizers, and other paraphernalia in the cases, there were also large containers filled with boutique marijuana varietals, known for their nuances in color, potency, flavor, and aroma—sort of like with wines. As patrons near us were shown the well-trimmed marijuana buds, the pungent and somewhat skunky smell reached our noses. It sure felt a bit surreal for me to be here with my mom.

But we were not here for the flowers or the edibles. We were interested in the products displayed on the shelves and hanging off hooks behind the counter—the medicinal marijuana products containing CBD.

"Hi, there," I opened. "This is my ninety-year-old mom, Norma, and she is interested in some of your CBD topical creams."

"Wow, we don't get many ninety-year-olds in here," our consultant replied. Visibly excited to see a wheelchair-bound old lady in the dispensary, she called one of her coworkers over to share the novelty and his product knowledge.

"Yes," I continued, "we are looking for a cream or lotion that might help with my mom's arthritis and this swelling of her leg." I glanced at Mom as she pulled her pant leg up a bit for emphasis.

Over the next half hour we asked dozens of questions and learned more than we thought possible about CBD products and their use. We were shown them in oil, tincture, and capsule form. We deliberated a bit before deciding to purchase a small sample bottle of extra-strength pain cream to try out on her leg and hands.

Since Mom was engaged and curious during our exchange about the CBDs and how they worked, I thought I would up the ante and suggest that we try this approach to her overall pain management. I told the two cannabis experts that we were thinking of replacing Mom's opioids with CBD capsules. They encouraged caution.

"We've seen that this stuff works for pain," said the male half of the duo, "but I would maybe take the CBD in addition to her normal medication for a while. You can slowly wean her off the opioid if you see that it's working."

"That sounds fine to me," Mom agreed.

We left the building with our cannabis cream and a bottle of five-milligram CBD capsules.

Mom rubbed some of the cannabis cream onto her swollen leg and into her gnarled hands just before her nine o'clock bedtime that same night. The next morning she could not wait to emerge from her bedroom to show us that her swelling had gone down significantly—at least 50 percent. We could see the wrinkles where the skin had shrunk. Her arthritic hands felt better too.

Mom also began taking the CBD capsules. We moved slowly at first, but she improved so much that in only a week she was able to stop taking the opioids completely. She had a few restless nights of sleep in the beginning, but soon one CBD capsule a day was keeping her more pain-free than her prescription. We were all elated.

Soon most of my mom's prescriptions had been responsibly disposed of. Her dizziness, lethargy, and runny nose were but a memory. Her pain was now managed better with none of the nasty side effects.

We are not medical experts, of course, but when it came to taking care of my ninety-year-old mom, we had to ask ourselves: How good was a medication if it took the joy out of her life? If it made her sleepy all day? If it offered her a laundry list of side effects in exchange for barely managed pain? Quality of life is a major issue that the medical community is just beginning to deeply grapple with. All we can say is that Mom's wish, from the moment of her initial diagnosis, was to experience as much of what life had to offer as she could. Our desire was simply to honor that however we could.

Four days after Mom began her CBD regimen, while I took Ringo for a walk, she whispered something to Ramie as if the walls were listening.

"I think I stopped bleeding," she said.

"Are you kidding?" Ramie replied.

Keeping her voice low, Mom continued, "I think we need to go back to that marijuana shop."

So we did.

CHAPTER 6

Dreams

JEMEZ PUEBLO, NEW MEXICO

NOVEMBER

[Ramie]

When we embarked on this journey, my mother-in-law could think of only one place in the country she wanted to make sure she saw: New Mexico. Everything else we could take day by day, but we knew we must eventually make it there. She could not tell us why the "Land of Enchantment" had enchanted her so. We were on a bit of a treasure hunt on that one.

We had just finished visiting Prescott and took Norma to experience the wonder of Grand Canyon National Park before heading east on I-40 toward Gallup, New Mexico. As we drove through the painted desert, we talked about possibly stopping at the National WWII Museum in New Orleans after our New Mexico stay and before making our way east to Florida for the winter. Norma was so excited to go to that museum that it got me thinking. Perhaps Norma's desire to see New Mexico stemmed from a single railroad trip she had made across the continent in 1945.

That year Norma was only twenty years old and leaving home for the first time in her life, on her way to serve as a nurse at the San Diego Naval Hospital. Before volunteering to serve in World War II, she had not been more than twenty miles from her home in Toledo.

I imagined a pretty, petite young woman leaning her stylish curly brown hair against the passenger car window as the troop train chugged through the barren desert landscape of the Southwest. Everything was unfamiliar; everything was new. Her moist young skin would have begun to feel dry and tight from the arid air. Her eyes would have collected visions of places and people she had only ever imagined through cowboy movies and picture books.

What had she seen? Did she ride through tribal land, the train tracks evidence of settler intrusions long ago? Did she spy adobe pueblos from that window? Perhaps Native American children played in the dirt as she rode past them, or mothers carried small children in colorfully woven papooses, the babies holding tightly to their mothers' long straight black hair.

Maybe she saw a brilliant golden sunrise as her train rattled down the tracks past Santa Fe to Albuquerque before continuing west to sun-drenched San Diego. Perhaps she sat in awe of the sharp angles of the vegetation-less landscape and the wide-open sky, which would have sharply contrasted with her hometown, a bustling industrial city defined by smokestacks and streetcars.

That trip had taken place over seventy years ago. I asked Norma about the journey, longing for every detail, but she could not recall much, except that she passed through without stopping. I could not blame her for not remembering; it was a long time ago. What we knew for sure was that New Mexico had imprinted itself on her. After all this time, it was our job to help her experience it.

◊ ◊ ◊

"How about Chaco Canyon?" I asked Norma. "Although the trails around the ancient ruins might be hard with the wheelchair. You might have to walk with your cane. But it looks really cool." As we drove along the highway, I brainstormed out loud all the great things New Mexico is known for and presented them for her consideration.

Norma was understandably hesitant about the physical exertion Chaco Canyon required. "I'm not sure I could walk it," she said.

We had already passed Gallup by now and were nearing the Coronado Campground in Bernalillo, New Mexico, which would be our base for the next few days. Our Baja California friend, Mark, was driving down from Durango, Colorado, to tent camp and spend a little time with us.

"Hmmm . . . Old Town Albuquerque might be fun," I tried again after we had parked. With each suggestion I hoped for a positive reaction from Norma. "There's a lot of history there as well as food and art to enjoy," I told her.

All that got me was another "Oh, I don't know."

The annual migration of thousands of sandhill cranes in the area was interesting to me from a photographer's point of view, but she was unmoved by that idea as well.

"What do you think of visiting the International UFO Museum in Roswell?" I thought she would enjoy a good giggle viewing the collected alien oddities.

"Well, maybe," she replied, her voice divulging her reluctance. There were so many options, but none seemed to be the right fit.

Of course! I thought that evening as I looked across the dinette at Tim. He was wearing a T-shirt Norma had given him from a Native American children's charity she had made small donations to over the years. It was just one of the many charities she had contributed to, and the T-shirt was a thank-you gift for her donation. "You would probably like to go see a Native American community, wouldn't you, Norma?"

It was the first idea that really sparked an interest. "Yes, I think I would really like that," she said.

I quickly began looking for a way to have a genuine experience with the culture she had for so long connected to from afar. The more we talked about it, the more it became clear: no tourist stop would do. She wanted to see real pueblo-style homes. She wanted to share a smile with the people. She wanted to take in the authentic smells and sounds of tribal living, appreciate their craftsmanship, and just quietly be with them. It was a tall order, for Native American communities are quite private and protected—for good reason. I did not think that sort of experience existed anymore, but I was willing to look into it further.

Online, I was able to learn that many pueblos have patron-saint or feast days. Traditional ceremonies and dances are generally closed to the public, but some Native American celebrations have strong Catholic elements—a result of Spanish attempts to forcibly Christianize the indigenous peoples. I found that these tribal communities sometimes welcomed visitors in to witness their Catholic-influenced patron-saint celebrations. I kept reading, trying to understand how the whole thing worked, and looked for the feast dates of nearby pueblos. When I came across a web page for the pueblo closest to us, I could not believe my eyes.

"Oh my! It's tomorrow! I can't believe it, it's tomorrow!" I yelled to Tim, Norma, and Mark, who had found our campsite and was now sitting with us in the motor home.

"What's tomorrow? What are you talking about?" everyone asked.

I realized I had been working on this plan for so long on the Internet that I had not yet shared any of this information with them. Tim had no idea what I was talking about. Neither did Norma or Mark.

"We are going to a place called Walatowa tomorrow!" I continued. Norma's ears perked up at my excitement. "Oh, this is so great!"

"I thought that was a closed pueblo. Are you sure?" Mark chimed in, knowing a bit more about the area than we did. "That's the Jemez tribe, right?" He was trying to temper my enthusiasm.

"The pueblo is closed three hundred sixty-four days a year, but *not* tomorrow! We're going! I am one hundred percent sure!" I could not contain myself. I just knew this had to be the experience Norma was hoping for but could not articulate for us. The look on her face confirmed it. "The annual Feast Day celebration of their patron saint, San Diego, is on November twelfth," I said, thinking specifics would help everyone believe me.

But Mark's and Tim's responses did not matter to me as much as Norma's did: "Wow." Which was all she needed to say. We were doing this.

"Walatowa," I learned in my online searching, was a Towa word meaning "this is the place." It seemed like destiny. Although the Walatowa Visitor Center on the highway was open for tourists, the Jemez Pueblo itself was closed to the public. But that November day visitors were welcome to attend a public dance. We were in exactly the right place at exactly the right time.

Our destination was only thirty minutes from our campground, but we still had no idea what we were getting into as we all climbed into the Jeep on that Feast Day. There were no photos available online and actually very little information about the event other than, thankfully, the etiquette for visiting a Native American community. The most relevant rule for me was "No photographs."

The state highway that bypasses the pueblo was relatively nondescript; it wound between the red sandstone mesas that dominated the horizon. As we left the pavement to enter the village, it was clear that something special was going on. Cars were parked everywhere along the narrow, bumpy streets, and groups of people were walking toward the main square. Typically, Norma's handicap parking placard would have afforded us a great parking spot, but not this time. We were going to have to hike for a while to get to the heart of the village.

I took a deep breath and left my camera in the car. Tim, Mark, and I took turns pushing and dragging Norma's wheelchair through the community. The white-sand lanes were soft and deep enough to swallow its tires. The smell of burning mesquite permeated the air with undertones of *tamales* and fry bread. In the distance, we could hear the unmistakable beat of ceremonial drums.

With no camera lens between me and my surroundings, I found myself desperately trying to capture every moment in my mind's eye, my human shutter constantly on motor drive. It took me a while to settle into being present. I felt myself breathing differently, a little slower and more relaxed. So far on this trip with Norma I thought we had been doing a good job of living in the moment. Now that I was forced to put down my "memory catcher," I could feel how much I had been trying to see life through Norma's eyes and not my own. I was bearing witness through my own aperture now.

The sand became so deep that we could not move anywhere quickly in the crowded village. Spontaneously, Mark and Tim reported to Norma and me, "We're going to check things out." And they were off. With a skip in their steps, like two eleven-year-old boys at a county fair suddenly liberated from their parents, they headed toward the drumbeats. This impulsive move also meant they were free from the wheelchair. Norma and I were stuck.

Luckily, it was not long before the guys returned, and they brought with them a wide-eyed look of excitement on their faces.

"We found out why we are here! Come on, Mom!" Tim and Mark each took a side of Norma's wheelchair and carried her like a queen in a sedan chair until they made it to firmer ground.

Around the next bend, we came to the center of the pueblo. Everything was beautiful in its simplicity; the colorful laundry hanging out to dry and family dogs roaming out front all let us know this was a neighborhood, not a living history exhibit.

Crowded rows of lawn chairs encircled the "main street" of the community, where we could see that hundreds of people were already settled in for the day. We noticed only a few white faces besides our own. As newcomers to the festivities, we would need to jockey for a good viewing spot. "We should have arrived a few hours ago." I sighed. "How is Norma ever going to see what's going on?"

But then something remarkable happened. No matter how entrenched people were in the spaces they had carved out for themselves, they quietly made room for Norma, the respected elder in the wheelchair. As we walked past, kind faces nodded hello and gently moved aside. I could not help but flash back to all the doctor's visits and tests Norma underwent just a few months ago. The kind of dignity and reverence expressed here for the elderly stood in stark contrast to Norma and Leo being treated as simply a medical problem to be solved.

Norma eventually found herself sitting comfortably at one end of the courtyard, front and center, while the three of us kneeled around her wheelchair. We watched as hundreds of tribal members, men and women, young and old, participated in the San Diego Feast Day dance. All were dressed in stunning traditional costumes. They danced in formation, each dancer stepping rhythmically to the beat of a few dozen drums and the chants of many men.

There was no applause at the end of each dance, for these people were dancing for reasons other than external reward. We were not at a show, but a spiritual celebration; we were not attending a performance, rather witnessing a meditation, a moving prayer, a connection to Mother Earth and Father Sky—a tradition passed down from their elders for generations.

In the presence of this holy dance, it struck me how powerful such traditions can be. Neither Tim nor I come from families rich in tradition or ritual. I was in awe of the intergenerational beauty, the commitment to culture, and the radiance of the people.

Norma seemed to agree. "This sure is something," she said to me with raised eyebrows as I knelt next to her.

Back at the campground a few hours later, we all remarked that our hearts felt like they were still beating to the rhythm of drums located some thirty miles to the north. Weary and sore from the excitement of the day, I sat on the motor-home floor next to Ringo and rested my legs as I listened to Tim, Mark, and Norma recall everything we had seen and heard. The twinkle in Norma's eyes made me think back to that young girl on the troop train. With her whole life ahead of her, Norma had sought adventure in service, traveling across the country into the unknown. And here she was, all these years later, sitting across from me on another set of wheels, a huge, exhausted smile brightening every wrinkle on her face, still traveling into parts unknown, on another adventure.

That night, at Norma's self-appointed nine o'clock bedtime, I held her right hand as her other hand wrapped around the head of her trusty cane. Out of nowhere, we both just began singing and dancing our way to the back of the motor home, and it felt good. We found ourselves doing it again the next night and the night after that too. Soon Tim starting joining in, and eventually this simple act became our unintentional family ritual, one we would repeat every night like a prayer. It took me a little while to understand that the gift of that day—the gift Norma had given us with her dream of experiencing authentic New Mexico—was this sudden and unplanned act, a daily celebration for our family who had had none.

CHAPTER 7

Healing

FORT MYERS BEACH, FLORIDA

DECEMBER

[Tim]

We all grieve differently, and for my parents, it was in absolute silence. I had longed to talk to them about Stacy ever since she died. My dad, especially, would not have anything to do with that topic, and it was generally considered "off-limits." We had no shared rituals to mourn, remember, or celebrate her. I never phoned home on her birthday or on the anniversary of her death for fear of upsetting either of them.

Now that Dad was no longer alive, I thought I might have a better chance speaking to Mom about Stacy. This trip was a reminder that we had recently added new layers of shared loss. Stacy's name was brought up from time to time during our travels when something reminded us of her. But still, these conversations were barely more than acknowledgments that she once had existed, not about any real feelings about her or her life. We seemed to be continuing our long family tradition of allowing grief to isolate us rather than bring us closer.

I was starting to give up hope of ever having a truly meaningful talk with Mom about our loss until Ramie and I met a couple in a hot tub late one afternoon while we were staying at an RV park in Fort Myers Beach, Florida.

The early evening sun was still warm but not intrusive, and the pool deck was empty except for the four of us. I could smell a strong whiff of rum coming from their tropical-themed Tervis Tumblers, and by the sound of their voices I could tell those were not their first drinks of the day.

"Where are you from?" we offered.

Rick and Jo did not smile much, but they were pleasant. We all shared where we were from and some details about our respective journeys. Ours, of course, revolved around my mom. Intrigued by our story, they invited us all out for a ride in their fancy jet boat the following day.

"We have to tell you something, though," they said.

It was then we learned why they were here in Florida: to spread the ashes of their two eldest sons. Only in their twenties, one had died of a heart attack and the other had taken his life not long after. Rick and Jo's sole remaining child, a nineteen-year-old son, was back at their motor home and would be coming along to share in the ceremony. That explained the lack of jocularity in the hot tub—and the sadness encircling Jo's kind blue eyes. These were people beset by grief. I felt a sort of kinship with them and shared that I had lost my sister when she was only forty-four and that my dad had recently died. My family had never had any kind of closure like this, I reflected.

We were unsure if Mom would be up for a boat ride. We told Rick and Jo that she probably would not.

"Well, I hope you said yes," Mom said after we told her of the offer, always surprising us with her desire for adventure. But would she be willing to mourn with this family—or at least be willing to witness their grief?

"There's a caveat," we told her. She listened carefully as we explained what was going to happen once we reached the open ocean. Never one to express herself in many words, she agreed to come along with a nod in the affirmative and a look on her face of deep empathy.

It was a wonderful day for a boat ride. We met Rick, Jo, and their son at the marina and eased Mom onto the boat through the open stern, sitting her on a heavily padded seat in the front. Rick carefully followed the marked channel on low throttle past the shrimp fleet and under the bridge until we reached the last marker and open water. Then he opened it up and propelled us at high speed to get beyond the surf at Fort Myers Beach. The wave tips beyond sparkled like diamonds in the full sun.

Rick cut the engine once we were well offshore, and we could see the white-sand beaches of Sanibel Island only a few miles distant. The boys' favorite song, "Drink a Beer" by Luke Bryan, played over the boat stereo, and the family laughed and cried, telling stories of each boy's life as we all toasted them with a beer of our own. They acknowledged their sons' accomplishments and their unique personalities with pride and love.

The ceremony was beautifully symbolic. Dolphins breached nearby and a double rainbow—to all of us representing the two brothers—appeared as their ashes were scattered overboard. Tenderly, subtly, Mom's tanned and wrinkled hand reached out to hold Jo's hand. In that moment, I believe I saw my mom's own healing begin.

◊ ◊ ◊

"No, no, no, that's not possible," Dad screamed as we sat together in the living room of Stacy's townhouse in Alexandria, Virginia. He and Mom had stayed behind at the house that April morning, waiting for word from me about my sister's latest surgery. I had been filled with dread during the half-hour drive from the hospital. After I had pulled up to Stacy's two-story Colonial and walked slowly toward her bright red front door, I braced myself to give them the news.

Just one year earlier, my sister's storied Secret Service career—and her life—had come crashing down after a routine visit to her dentist. He had seen a white spot on the bottom of her tongue that troubled him enough to make an appointment for her to see an oncologist. As they say: the rest is history.

For Stacy, that included a wasted year of surgeries, radiation, and chemotherapy. I was my sister's caregiver after the first surgery, to remove part of her tongue and the lymph nodes on her left side. She was a gourmet and had just finished remodeling her kitchen a few days before that fateful dental appointment. Taking away her ability to eat and taste food seemed to me to be a cruel trick. I then watched helplessly as the strongest person I knew in the world was slowly reduced to the frail being my parents and I had seen lying in the hospital bed during this, the last week of her life, hooked up to monitors, feeding tubes, and a catheter, unable to speak.

"I'm sorry, Dad," I said, "but it is true." I reached out to put my arm around his small shoulders, but he jumped up from the couch and pushed me away before I could comfort him.

Our family had been summoned from different parts of the country only days before by my sister. She must have known even before the doctors did that she was near the end of her struggle. It was confirmed a little more than an hour earlier when I looked up from the magazine I was reading in the crowded hospital waiting room to find Stacy's surgeon standing in front of me. Seeing the doctor in her dirty scrubs and with her mask hanging loosely around her neck, I felt like I was in the middle of a network-television medical drama.

"Your sister's cancer is rapidly spreading," she said flatly. "I'm afraid there is nothing more we can do for her."

The words hit me hard. Just a few hours earlier, I had been holding Stacy's hand as she was being prepped for surgery. Hers had been the first of nine operations that day for Dr. Lee, and I had watched with hope as my sister was pushed through the double doors leading to the surgical rooms beyond. "Everything is going to be okay, Stacy," I had told her as the doors had noise-lessly swung shut behind her.

"Are you sure, Dr. Lee?" I barely managed to ask.

"Yes. She has only a few more days," she replied, a slight crack in her voice betraying the emotions hiding behind her ordinarily professional demeanor. She was sad to have lost the battle too, I suspected, having spent a lot of time treating Stacy during the past year.

I began to quietly sob, my chest heaving as I tried to hold back the tears that streamed down my cheeks anyway. And then I wailed, anguish washing over me in relentless waves. Everyone in the waiting room uncomfortably glanced my way. I could see the nervousness in their eyes as each convulsive gasp of my lungs made manifest their worst fears. My worst fears too.

Someone called a grief counselor, and I was ushered into her office out of earshot of the others. The counselor did her best to console me. I dried my eyes with several tissues from a box that was conveniently located on the corner of her desk, and began slowly regaining my composure. But grief overcame me again when I realized that I was the one who had to give my parents the terrible news.

I called Ramie from the hospital parking lot and told her what had happened. "How am I going to tell my mom and dad this?" I asked weakly. "This is just going to kill them."

"You have to be strong, Tim," Ramie replied. "Your sister is depending on you to be the strong one now." Deep down, I knew she was right.

Mom just sat there on the couch, her already tiny frame diminished with grief after I shared the news. Dad continued to pace the room, shouting and in complete denial of what he had heard. I had delivered news that no parent wants to hear: they would be outliving their only daughter.

◊ ◊ ◊

In my twentieth year, I packed up my dark blue Datsun B210 hatchback with all my worldly possessions and drove across the country's midsection to start a new life in the Colorado Rockies. The extreme July heat during the twelve-hundred-mile trip challenged my enthusiasm, especially since my little foreign car was not equipped with air-conditioning. Although I did not know anyone living in the Centennial State, I knew that I truly belonged there after just a brief ten-day visit with an old girlfriend the previous year. Thinking solely about the new life ahead of me, I avoided looking back.

Stacy was only thirteen years old when I moved out West, and she finished growing up in a house in Ohio that my parents bought after I had left home. She liked to watch television cartoons after doing her household chores. She would dress up in costumes, mixing genres but always equipping herself with toy weapons, like a gun or sword—or both. She played the flute and later was in the high school marching band.

I did not make it back home much in those days and I rarely spent time thinking about my family. We spent a holiday or two together over the next years, but the occasions were few because I no longer had a car or much money while I was completing my degree at the University of Colorado at Boulder. In fact, my situation was so tight during that time that I had to reverse the charges whenever I made one of my infrequent calls home from a pay phone.

My first wife and I met in college, and we were married several years after we both graduated. It was at our mountain wedding, in the shadow of Longs Peak, that I first greeted my sister as an adult. She was twenty-two years old and had just been commissioned in the U.S. Army as a second lieutenant because of her college ROTC studies.

When she arrived with my parents she was wearing her dress uniform—skirt, collared shirt, jacket, and a beret. I barely recognized her. We did not have much time to catch up before the ceremony, and she left the reception early to take Dad down to a lower elevation because the altitude at our alpine venue made it hard for him to breathe. It was nearly ten more years before I truly had a chance to have an adult relationship with her.

And what a life she packed into those years. She spent her four-year military commitment as an explosive ordnance disposal expert. Like our mom, she broke gender stereotypes when she volunteered for this dangerous work, which entailed taking bombs apart. She also trained with the U.S. Navy SEALs in order to have the diving skills necessary to dismantle a nuclear warhead from a sunken submarine. Her final test was to deactivate a mock missile on a scuttled submarine at an undisclosed location near the mouth of the murky Potomac River. Later, while stationed in Vicenza, Italy, she spent her workdays dismantling terrorist bombs, from Northern Ireland to Israel. In her free time, she rode her high-performance Ducati motorcycle at high speeds through the Italian Alps.

"Did you ever get blown up?" I asked her later in life after noticing she no longer had hair on her forearms.

"Yeah, once," she nonchalantly answered. "It blew me a hundred feet in the air."

"Did you ever tell Mom or Dad about this?"

"Nope."

Stacy and Dad were always two peas in a pod. As much time as I spent in the kitchen cooking or helping Mom with painting, building her a potting shed, or working on her list of repair projects over the years, Stacy spent at gun shows with our dad, talking cars and getting him wound up with her crazy stories. Even so, it did not surprise me that when she received the cancer diagnosis, she did not immediately tell my parents. This response was typical of my family: what you don't know won't hurt you.

Her job dedication after four years was not enough to get her promoted to the rank of captain. In fact, Stacy was passed over several times in favor of male colleagues. She realized then that she had already hit the army's glass ceiling.

Around this same time my sister met several United States Secret Service special agents, when she was tasked with screening some of President Ronald Reagan's gifts. They saw potential in her and encouraged her to apply to the Service, which was actively recruiting women at the time. When her enlistment was up, my sister quit the army and returned stateside to apply.

She lived with my dad's brother in Toledo and worked as a factory night watch for nearly a year while her security clearance was processed. Stacy was the first adoptee ever considered by the Secret Service. Each member of the family, including both of our birth parents, had to be thoroughly vetted to be sure she was not a mole from a foreign country. We must have all passed muster, because she became a special agent in 1990.

My sister rose through the ranks fast. During her first assignment at the Toledo Field Office, she investigated counterfeit and fraud cases, consistently making twice the number of arrests as the other three agents combined. Only two years into her career, she was assigned to protect a young Arkansas governor who was running for president.

By 1992, I had been living in Hawaii for five years and had not seen Stacy for quite some time. I called her to catch up on things and to see how life on the road with a presidential candidate was going. The political season was in full swing by then, and Bill Clinton's face was on every television newscast.

"How come I never see you protecting this guy, Stacy?" I teased. "He's on television all the time."

"I'm there. You just can't see me," she replied. "It's my job not to be noticed."

"Yeah, right," I sarcastically retorted.

"Okay, I'll tell you what," she said. "Watch the national news tonight and look for me."

That night I followed my sister's instructions and faithfully watched the evening news. There it finally was: Clinton's three minutes of coverage for that day. It was a tight camera shot of the candidate standing behind a podium, with nothing discernible in the background but an American flag. But wait, what was that I just saw? Leaning into and out of view on national television with the ease of a seasoned photo bomber was my straight-faced sister!

When my marriage started to fail a short time later, I telephoned Stacy more and more to talk and receive moral support. Having a little sister dispense advice and protect her big brother certainly seemed a reversal of the traditional roles. She was the strong, grounded one with the heavyweight career, and she was certainly better suited to that position than I was.

My divorce became final not long after, and I was forced to leave everything in Hawaii and try to start my life all over again on the mainland. But where could I go to do that? All the years of my unintentional family estrangement were put behind me in an instant when I realized that I literally had nowhere to go. I had to ask my sister. Although we had spent little time together as adults, Stacy did not hesitate to invite me to move in with her at her new place for as long as I needed.

"You realize that this is a one-way ticket to Newark, New Jersey?" the agent behind the United Airlines counter incredulously asked. I was at Honolulu International Airport checking in the two large duffel bags that held all my post-divorce possessions. "It's the end of February, and it still has to be cold there," she added.

"Yeah, I know," I mumbled.

My sister had just been transferred to the Newark Field Office (actually located in Morristown, New Jersey, because apparently Newark was too dangerous even for the Secret Service), and she had arrived only a few weeks before I did. Moving-company boxes of every size greeted me as I walked into her two-level condominium, subdivided from an old Morristown mansion and just blocks from headquarters.

I showed up with practically nothing: no car, no job, no friends, and no self-esteem. The divorce had taken all those things from me. I spent time unpacking my sister's belongings and integrating them into her new place. I also spent time unpacking some emotional baggage I had brought along. Stacy and I would share a beer at the end of the day when she came home from work and we would both unwind. Her job was understandably a stressful one, even when she was not physically guarding the president.

The World Wide Web was still in its infancy, but already criminals were figuring out ways to exploit it for their own benefit. My sister's interest in computers got her involved in the Secret Service's nascent Electronic Crimes Task Force. She was working on a computer bulletin board sting dubbed Operation Cybersnare when I left her and New Jersey a few months later. Her efforts would eventually culminate in arrests in seven states and the breakup of a three-billion-dollar-a-year sophisticated cell-phone fraud ring.

Stacy spent the last eleven years of her Secret Service career in Washington, DC, in various positions. During that time she led fifteen foreign and nine domestic presidential advance details, some in difficult countries, such as India, Uganda, and Nicaragua. She was as comfortable smoking cigars with former Sandinista rebels in the mountains of Nicaragua as she was meeting kings, presidents, heads of state, or the pope. She was as tough as nails. She was a true badass. She was my hero.

And I lost her. We all did, but we never spoke of it. In fact, it felt like we lost her twice: once when she died and again through our silences, which allowed the story of her life to die too. We did not fill the space she left with remembrances; instead we allowed her absence to box us into our private grief.

My dad gave no hospital-bed confession of his feelings about Stacy's death. Every opportunity I had to push him to open up about her over the years was effectively squandered. He left this world unable to talk about it. Did Mom want to talk about her beloved daughter? Had she remained silent because Dad had been so heartbroken?

Much as I had wanted to talk about Stacy with my parents, I had been distant too. It was our collective fault. When we did come together, we did so easily enough, but we each had our barriers. The conversations we had—like so many families just trying to get along—lacked real substance. Stacy's death blew a hole through so many of the walls I had built between my family and me, but even that had not been enough. Mom and I had no model for being together in a state of such raw emotion, no map to show us how to bridge the lonely path of grief and pain. That is, until we met Rick and Jo.

◊ ◊ ◊

For the rest of our three-week stay in Fort Myers Beach, Ramie and I would come back from our morning beach walks with Ringo to find Mom and Jo sitting in our screen house outside the motor home talking. We left them be. They were two mothers in a club that no parent wants to belong to. Sometimes they would sit quietly together, but other times the warm Florida breeze carried their voices in through the open windows. We heard them bonding over grief, resolve, and faith.

Rick and Jo were real with their grief. There was no pretense, no need to seem strong or to fear expressing the messy disorientation of sorrow. This journey so far had given us a special kind of familial joy: we had seen my mom's smile for the first time in years, her silliness, and her sense of adventure. But we were still experts at avoiding the hard stuff. Rick and Jo showed us that it was possible to grieve as a family as well. The authenticity of their sadness and their remembering showed us that if we let go of trying to keep things "okay" on the surface, we might be gifted with feeling more—more pain, yes, but also more connection and love, the only true antidotes to sorrow.

Watching my mom with Jo, I understood that we all speak our own emotional languages. Perhaps sharing grief with Mom did not mean that we cried together but instead meant something more subtle: the touch of a hand, a mutual expression of faith, locking eyes for a moment to say *"I see you and what you are going through."* I still had not known Mom to shed a tear for my sister's death or my dad's, but that day on the boat, and later in the soft murmuring of these mothers' voices, I felt a shift in her. The pain in her heart began tiptoeing out from the safe place where it had been hiding, wrapping itself in Jo's warm embrace. And I knew that if my mom could begin to heal, then I could too. We could do it together.

CHAPTER 8

Flight

ORLANDO, FLORIDA

JANUARY

[Ramie]

When Tim and I first met, I shared two nonnegotiables with him that we still embrace today. One was a promise that we would make all our decisions out of love, not fear; the other was that we would live a life free of regrets. "No woulda, coulda, shoulda," I told him. It was the mantra of our marriage; now it was also the mantra of our nursing home on wheels.

After Tim and I discovered all the newspaper advertisement clippings in July, we secretly made a pact: we were going to take Norma on a hot-air balloon ride. But it was a goal that proved harder to reach than we initially thought. As we made our way through our country's West and Southwest, I looked into the prospect again and again, but no hot-air balloon options in our projected travel path were accessible to the elderly.

November came and went, and the Christmas holiday was fast approaching, but I was still coming up empty in my search. Some companies would take her up in a balloon tethered to the ground, but this felt wrong to me—she needed to fly! Others offered untethered flights, but they had no seats in the basket. This was important because I knew my mother-in-law did not have the strength to stand for over an hour. But even if I found a hot-air balloon with a seat, I still had no idea how she would get into the basket. She certainly could not use the basket's foot holes to climb in by herself.

Were there accessible balloons? Did a balloon basket exist that had a door where we could push her wheelchair in? I had more questions than answers. I imagined all sorts of scenarios: Maybe she could sit on a barstool inside the basket so she could see over the sides. Would that be safe? But I always returned to the problem of getting her in. I scoured the Internet and called around, and I kept hitting dead ends. We were not only limited by Norma's physical state; we also had only an approximate idea of where we would be in the country and when.

Since we knew we would probably spend the whole winter in Florida, I zeroed in on the Sunshine State. Seated in our screen tent at a quiet campsite in Henderson Beach State Park near Destin, Florida, I feverishly jotted down phone numbers and began making calls while Ringo napped at my feet.

After several balloon companies failed to answer the phone, one hot-air balloon outfit finally picked up on the first ring.

"Thompson Aire! This is Jeff. How may I help you?" a voice boomed through my cell phone.

"My mother-in-law is ninety and I would like to find a way to get her into a hot-air balloon. I saw that you have a balloon with seats and I would like to learn more about that, but first, am I crazy to even consider this adventure?" I blurted out all in one breath, but soon I relaxed into a chat with this friendly man and his warm customer service.

As I was speaking with Jeff, Dr. Gawande's thoughts about safety and autonomy were on my mind. "That our most cruel failure in how we treat the sick and the aged is the failure to recognize that they have priorities beyond merely being safe and living longer; that the chance to shape one's story is essential to sustaining meaning in life," he wrote in his book *Being Mortal*. I remembered saying "*Yes!*" to myself when I first read that passage so many months before. But I also really wanted to hear Jeff say all the right things so I could trust that we would not be putting Norma in harm's way and that her story would be shaped positively.

The vibration of Jeff's enthusiasm for ballooning carried through our cellular connection. With an excited note in his voice and a reassuring tone of confidence, he rattled off his ballooning résumé from the time he was fifteen years old and indicated that he and his family were capable of making our dream for Norma come true. His most recent accomplishment, he shared, was completing the highest pilot achievement level obtainable by the Balloon Federation of America—one of only thirty-two pilots in the United States to do so. I could tell that he had a passion for ballooning, and he assured me that he was up for the challenge our family presented. *This might really happen,* I allowed myself to think.

Jeff described his safety record in detail and then got to the good stuff: "Our balloons are different from most. They have bench seats, so Norma will ride comfortably. No problem."

We had made it over the first hurdle with the seat. I took a deep breath before I asked my next question. "But how will she get into the basket?"

"Don't worry about that, Ramie. It will happen. I promise," Jeff assured me like an old friend. "I recently got a six-hundred-fifty-pound man up in one of our balloons, and you say your mother-in-law is as light as a feather. She will definitely fly." So I scheduled a date, and Tim and I came up with a plan.

Christmas was only a few days away, so we decided to surprise Norma on Christmas morning with the news. "God, I hope she still wants to do this," I told Tim as we searched the local grocery store for crafting supplies. As typically frugal travelers, we generally did not splurge on costly diversions such as hot-air balloon rides, but we had convinced ourselves it would be money well spent.

My worry was soon overcome by childlike excitement as Tim and I fashioned a children's punch balloon and some construction paper into a makeshift hot-air balloon with a little masking tape. Tim made a "ride voucher" and I tucked it into the home-made woven basket. We wanted to make a fuss; the balloon ride was an homage to Norma and Leo, after all, a dream that had long waited to be fulfilled.

As excited as any parent on Christmas morning, Tim and I tiptoed around the motor home, whispering and giggling to ourselves as we rushed to hang our hot-air balloon over Norma's seat at the dinette table before she arose. At nine A.M. sharp, Norma slid open her bedroom door, wearing a Santa hat just as Leo always had on Christmas Day. Instead of "We Wish You a Merry Christmas" playing on the stereo, we had "Up, Up and Away" by the 5th Dimension queued up.

The crescendo of the string instruments and the classic 1960s harmonizing lifted our already eager moods. Norma shuffled her way to the front of the motor home while Tim and I began singing softly along with the recording. By the end of the unlikely holiday tune, we were belting out "*Up, up, and away!*" at the top of our lungs.

"What's all this?!" Norma asked, a touch of enchantment in her voice. She settled into her seat and pulled the note from our hot-air-balloon replica's basket. "What *is* this?" she asked again.

We waited for her to read it. Big smiles were on our faces and my feet were tapping on the floor as I tried in vain to be patient. Tim was squeezing my hand under the table.

"We are really going to go on a hot-air balloon ride?" she said as she clasped her hands under her chin in delight.

"We are!" I responded.

"Oh wow," she said. "I can hardly believe it!"

Over breakfast, we had to keep confirming to Norma that we were indeed going up in a hot-air balloon. "January twentieth is the big day!" I assured her. She seemed completely dazzled and in awe of the fact that she was really going to fly.

"I think we made the right decision to splurge on this experience," I said to Tim later that day, after all the merriment had settled down and the sun had set. I could not keep from smiling as I said it. I was thinking back on Norma's surprise and the joy in her eyes.

"Yes, I think we did."

◊ ◊ ◊

It would be several more weeks and several more campgrounds around Florida's perimeter before we arrived in Orlando for the balloon ride. Since we had not been able to plan ahead for wintering in Florida, we were not able to settle in one place for the duration. But Stacy had answered the prayer I had made to her in August; over the course of the winter we managed to cobble together eight different RV parks, state parks, and wildlife preserves solely through other people's cancellations. It was a week here, three weeks here, four days there. And at every stop, Norma sent out postcards saying, "I'm going on a hot-air balloon ride on January 20th!"

As delighted as I was by Norma's gleeful anticipation, I held my breath every time she posted another card, because I feared that ultimately we might not be able to go; the weather would be wrong that day, her health might not be great, or maybe we would not be able to get her moving in the right direction that early in the morning. *Stop,* I told myself. *Worry, fear, doom, and gloom are all an absolute waste of energy. I know this. I live by this.*

We toasted the New Year with Rick and Jo in Fort Myers Beach, and by mid-January we were on our way to Lake Magic RV Resort near Orlando. The campground was filled with "snowbird" retirees spending their winter months in the temperate climes of central Florida. These folks were definitely a fair-weather bunch; everyone seemed to own an electric golf cart equipped with a zippered plastic enclosure to keep the typically wet winter weather out. The number of these "bubbles" driving around the park kept increasing, all of the occupants trying to keep the rain at bay.

And, boy, did it rain. In the first weeks of January we saw rain, wind, rain, and more rain. Each day my fears about the balloon ride crept in, and each day I practiced letting them go. Norma was not fazed at all. She continued to send out postcards.

On our appointed day, we woke to a crisp, dark morning. The sky was clear except for a few wispy clouds and the wind was calm. I could not believe it—it was the perfect day for a hot-air balloon ride. Later we learned that all hot-air balloon flights three days before and three days after our date had been canceled because of inclement weather. But on January 20, all was ideal.

Norma arose way before the sun, much earlier than her usual wake-up time. She dressed quickly, layering herself against the morning damp. She and Tim enjoyed a quick cup of decaffeinated coffee on the way out the door, but we all skipped breakfast, knowing that an all-you-can-eat brunch would follow our balloon ride. In the predawn light, we drove the ten minutes to our designated meeting spot in a restaurant parking lot, leaving Ringo behind to sleep some more.

A charming British man named Glenn greeted us after we had parked and had worked to get Norma out of the Jeep. At six feet five inches, he easily towered a foot and a half over Norma's petite frame. As she stepped off the stool we always carried in the Jeep, Glenn gave Norma a big smile. "I'm ready to lend a hand wherever needed," he reassured us.

Following close behind Glenn was the entire Thompson family. Jeff and his brother Jon were the pilots of the balloons launching that morning. The three of us would fly with Jon, while two other couples would go with Jeff. Their mom and dad were along too, serving with Glenn as the ground crew. While none of them quite rivaled Glenn in stature, they all equaled his enthusiasm. "Welcome to your dream adventure!" we heard them say again and again as they met us.

We quickly signed our lives away on some liability waivers and then were whisked into a van, with the company's colorful logo on the side, and off to the launch site.

When the sun finally rose, it painted the blue sky with brilliant yellow, pink, and, later, orange striations. We found ourselves parked at an open field about twenty minutes from our meeting place. The ground crew was already busy unloading the baskets and other equipment from two trailers by the time we arrived. Tim and I approached the smaller of the two baskets, assuming that one was ours.

The fire from the propane tanks hissed as the flames leaped toward the opening of the giant nylon drape. Norma remained inside the van, her eyes illuminated with excitement that rivaled the spectacle while her teeth chattered in the chilly January air. Tim was beaming as he busied himself by helping the ground crew with the inflation of our balloon. I did what I do best: I took lots of photographs, hoping for one good shot.

The once-wrinkled pile of nylon slowly grew to the size of a seven-story building right before our eyes. The balloon's rainbow stripes now seemed to pull the color from the brilliant sunrise as it became the grandest splendor visible in the morning sky.

"We're all set, Norma. Are you ready?" Connie, Jeff's mom, sang through the van's open side door.

"Okay, but how am I going to get in?" Norma worried aloud. "I can't lift my legs up high enough to climb in. Are you sure I will be able to go?"

Just then Glenn walked toward her. She looked more diminutive than ever next to the hulking Englishman. He bent over, locked his gorgeous blue eyes with Norma's, and said in his charming British accent, "Can I have a big hug?" Before she knew it, Norma was laughing uncontrollably as he lifted her up, carried her a few steps, and, as she later put it, "plopped" her into the wicker basket.

Once settled, and after recovering from deep belly laughter, we did a final safety review and then we were ready to take flight. This was my third experience in a hot-air balloon, but standing there in that basket, I knew this time I would spend more of the trip watching my dear mother-in-law than anything else. I found myself trying to crawl inside her eyes, to see things from her perspective, and to more accurately feel what she was feeling.

My mind flashed back to the rough edges of the one-column-inch hot-air balloon advertisement that had floated from Leo's book when we were sorting through his things. Then to the one that had also gone unnoticed for years, attached to the refrigerator by a magnet from the dentist. Another clipping had been lost in a tax file as recently as 2014.

Dr. Gawande's reflections came echoing back to me too—not so much in words but in feeling. All the fears that had been building up since Tim and I had made our pact to take Norma up in a hot-air balloon started to melt away. In the light of Norma's eyes I could see how truly beautiful it was to shape your own story, and how, facing the end of life, it might be a meaningful experience, not safety, that takes the lead. As we gently left the ground, I saw Norma take an extra breath. Maybe one to share with Leo, I thought. Or maybe she wanted to drink in the moment more deeply.

The balloon lifted us high into the sky, and Norma's eyes sparkled with an expression of delight. In wonder, with her lips parted and her cheeks rosy red, she looked up at the burner that heated the air lifting us. Then, gazing out at the still-rising sun and down at the treetops, her face relaxed more than I had ever seen it, a look of joy and peace radiating across her features as we climbed farther in elevation. I did not dare ask what she thought at that moment. It was her moment, not mine. I allowed myself to sink into a comfortable silence with my flying companions, weightlessness lifting me into deep, wordless contentment.

We drifted effortlessly through the morning sky. We floated over the contrived perfection of Walt Disney World, over a manicured golf course with Mickey Mouse–shaped sand traps, and over the rush-hour traffic on the roadways. Every time the propane-fueled burner blasted a flame just above our heads I felt a puff of love expanding in my chest, immune to the chaos below.

It was Norma who broke the silence. Her gloved hands lay gently on the leather-wrapped edge of the basket and her knitted prayer shawl covered her head and shoulders. The bright sun illuminated her face. She was glowing inside and out, just like the balloon. She looked up at Tim, a huge smile on her face, and she said, "Dad would have liked this."

CHAPTER 9

Impact

SAINT AUGUSTINE BEACH, FLORIDA

FEBRUARY

[Ramie]

In the early hours of a bright clear morning in late February, Tim and I lay on our inflatable mattress in the front of the motor home, scrolling through emails and Facebook messages. Ringo jumped into bed with us, making our situation more cramped than usual. We had settled into the Bryn Mawr Ocean Resort, tucked behind the dunes overlooking the Atlantic Ocean on Florida's northern coast. We could hear waves lapping on the beach and birds calling out to each other. We both had tears in our eyes.

"Is it possible for one heart to be able to hold all of this love?" Tim asked me.

In just a few short weeks our circle of influence had expanded so much that it now spanned the entire United States—and the whole world. On the one hand, most folks at the RV community where we were staying kept to themselves, and aside from a few labradoodle owners who felt a kinship with Ringo, we had not made many connections here like we had at some of our other stops. We were quite anonymous. On the other hand, emails and messages were now pouring into our Facebook and email accounts by the thousands from people who had heard about our story. It was surreal.

We read every single message.

A housebound woman in Connecticut wrote to thank Norma for inspiring her to finally leave the house and start her life anew.

An oncology nurse in a cancer hospital wrote to tell us she wished more terminal elderly patients would forgo invasive and debilitating treatment and enjoy their final days in peace. Traditional medical wisdom might offer them a few more days, she said, but in her experience, "not any more joy."

A family wrote to tell us that they had scheduled a 14-day, 6,300-mile road trip together after they read about Miss Norma. "We want to live while we can," they said.

A man in Perth, Western Australia, sent his blessings. Someone in Argentina sent a hug. Someone who had recently lost his grandmother wrote to ask if he could call Norma "Grammy." It went on and on and on.

Tim had not been exaggerating. Our hearts were so full they might burst at any moment. We had the support of so many people around the world, and that was breathing new energy into our days. But there was something else going on too. Here were so many people pouring out their deepest fears, losses, and desires to us. They told us of their caregiving struggles, their diagnoses, or their regrets. They shared with us their innermost desires—to finally plan that dream trip, to make peace with their recently deceased father, or to tell someone "I love you."

We had suddenly and dramatically found ourselves in the middle of an international conversation about the meaning of life, illness, aging, and love. We were learning on the fly how to open ourselves to holding so much raw emotion.

But that was not how it was at first. At first we were wrought with anxiety and panic, terrified of losing ourselves in a wave of publicity and responsibility.

◊ ◊ ◊

The number was 520. That was how many Facebook page "likes" we had at the six-month point of our trip. They were mostly from family, friends, and nice folks we had met along the way in campgrounds, in line at food trucks, and cruising around national parks.

At about the two-month mark we had been sitting at 83 "likes" until our friend Susan decided to campaign for us to hit 100. She begged everyone she knew to "like" our page, and we promised we would send a postcard from the Rocky Mountains to the hundredth person. We were not desperate for the ego boost, but okay, triple digits would be nice to see.

Our journey was hard sometimes. The photographs and happy times were all real, but full-time caregiving, no matter the circumstances, is not all rainbows and butterflies. Our lifestyle had changed significantly. Although Tim and I were still living a nomadic life, with Norma along we were not spending our time in the same ways. Instead of rising before the sun to hike for ten or twelve miles in a national park somewhere, we were waiting for her to rise and then looking for wheelchair-accessible routes to interesting sights, hoping Norma would find joy in the adventure. We worried about how much she ate and if she was sleeping enough. If Norma felt good and energetic, we would plan an outing. If not, we would settle in and read or do puzzles. She was our primary concern, her moods and health informing all we did.

When either Tim or I started to get "down in the dumps," to feel overwhelmed by caregiving, or even to question our decision to give up some of the freedom we had created in our lives to this point, we looked to the dozen or so people who had taken the time to "like" a post or comment on Facebook. Although they could not have known, those early supporters were our cheering section. They kept us going when we thought we could go no more.

So it was on a windy morning in Saint Augustine Beach, Florida, that I decided to write to one of our few Internet news sources, the Good News Network (GNN). On any given day, the "likes" and supportive comments from our 520 Facebook followers boosted our mood so much that I was inspired to spread the love a little more. I thought that maybe the GNN could post our story and reach more people.

A few days later I received an email requesting an interview. Before replying, I checked in with Norma and Tim.

"Honey, I'm not keen on this publicity thing," Tim was quick to say. "I'm a private guy, and besides, nobody is going to really care, no one who isn't following us already. Our circle of friends already knows what's going on. Do we really need to do this?" After a pregnant pause and some more thought, seeing the excitement in my eyes and perhaps remembering my need to make a difference in the world, he continued, "I guess we can see how it goes. But you aren't giving them our last names, are you? If no one reads it, no one reads it, right?"

"Right," I concurred, secretly hoping that would not be the case.

Norma simply said, "Do you think it'll be okay?"

"I don't have any way of knowing," I told her. "But what we put out there is all the truth, and we have seen that others have been inspired by your story. Look at the 520 people who have been following along. We probably don't even know 520 people altogether."

"Ain't that the truth," Norma quipped back.

"You are giving people hope and putting a smile on their faces. I bet there are more people who would feel good reading about you. I think it's nice to spread some joy out to the world."

"True," she agreed.

Together we looked at a few stories on the GNN page. We read "Shelter Surprises Homeless Couple with Fairy Tale Wedding," "WWII Vet Meets Girlfriend After 70 Yrs. Thanks to Strangers Funding Reunion," and "Boy with Cerebral Palsy Runs the Skate Park in a Wheelchair."

"Now, that sure is nice." Norma's interest in the page grew and we agreed that the world could use some more good news.

"It will just be a little article for the Good News Network. It won't be a big deal." I continued, "But with that said, I won't do the interview if you don't want to. It is one hundred percent your call, Norma."

She agreed, with my help, to answer the three emailed interview questions.

We sat together in the motor home's dinette, a little giddy at the idea of what we were doing.

"Does Norma have any advice for our readers about dealing with loss?" read one question.

"Keep praying every day and God will take care of you, even when it feels like you can't care for yourself," she answered.

"What's Norma's advice on staying positive?"

Never one to be long-winded, she said, "Just keep on going every day. That's about it."

"How do you deal with losing the love of your life?"

And in an answer that I knew was inspired by Rick and Jo back in Fort Myers Beach, she responded, "Storytelling is really, really helpful."

The following Sunday a chirp on my cell phone alerted me to a new email message. It was the GNN writing to let us know they had just posted the "Driving Miss Norma" story and hoped that we liked the way the story was presented. In addition to the three questions and answers, I had shared many of my photographs with the interviewer. I opened my computer to see that the GNN had done a wonderful job, and it was interesting to see our story through a lens other than our own. After that, our Facebook page began to blow up in front of our eyes. We quickly gained 30 new followers in less than an hour! Then it jumped to 637. Each time I refreshed the page, the number grew by leaps and bounds. By dinnertime we had 1,800 page "likes." When we finally went to bed that night, we had received a message to call the *CBS Evening News* in New York—they wanted to do a feature story.

We had plans to spend the next day touring Saint Augustine's Castillo de San Marcos with longtime family friends who were in the area and had met us there. But instead of learning about Spain's influence in early Florida with the rest of the group, I leaned against a cannon atop the 321-year-old fort talking with Courtney, a CBS News producer in New York City.

"As of five minutes ago, your Facebook 'likes' total 4,000. Did you have any idea this would happen?" Courtney asked.

As I stood there with my cell phone in one hand, the other hand up against my ear so I could better hear over the wind and the mob of fifth graders on a class trip, I could honestly say that I did not have the slightest idea any of this would happen. Nor did I have a clue about what was to come.

I spoke with Courtney for about forty-five minutes. We talked about hot-air balloons, dolphins, death, the Grand Canyon, cancer, and the spirit of a cute little lady who was unintentionally touching hearts around the country. Courtney was genuine and down-to-earth, someone I could easily imagine having over for dinner. At the same time, I was aware that this conversation might change all our lives. Out of a desire for authenticity, which had been the driving force behind so much of our journey, I blurted out, "I must tell you, Courtney, Norma is very shy and I honestly don't know if she will make 'good TV.' If it doesn't make sense to do this story we will not be heartbroken. She is our priority, not any kind of notoriety."

No commitments were made at the end of our conversation. Courtney needed to "talk to her people," and I certainly needed to talk to mine. I could not agree to a network television interview without having a family conference.

"In case you are wondering," Courtney said as we made our good-byes, "you are at 5,200 likes. Hold on for the ride! We'll talk soon."

The Facebook numbers kept growing. The people at GNN informed us that its "Driving Miss Norma" piece was its most-viewed feature story with more than 50,000 hits; the next popular was "Help Wanted: Professional Panda Cuddlers Needed in

China." How could Miss Norma possibly be more popular than a litter of cute panda babies?

But as those numbers grew, so did our anxiety. In fact, Tim and my collective feelings were more akin to fear than to excitement.

Five years before, when Tim and I decided to go media-free, we had done so because we wanted to choose what we allowed in, rather than passively absorbing all the messages that came our way. The onslaught of negative coverage—with its terrorism and gun violence, politics and scandals—had become too much. It had preyed on our nerves and had begun to influence our thinking. So we stopped watching the news and quit reading newspapers and magazines. We even blocked hard news from our Facebook feeds.

Now we were the news. And even more than that—now there were hundreds of people writing to and calling us, asking us to allow them into our lives.

My audacity has wrecked our lives, I lamented as each new request or "like" came in. I had robbed my family of its privacy. Norma's and Tim's trust in me had been eviscerated. I had created a monster that I did not know how to control. Even hearing the sound of my heartbeat while lying in bed at night made me uneasy.

Tim was mad. Really mad. "You had to have known this would happen," he said over and over. "We need to stop posting. Delete the Facebook page and make it go away. We can't do this. Mom can't do this."

What had I done?

◊ ◊ ◊

Messages continued to roll in by the thousands every hour, and we struggled to keep up with them all. We also began to realize that this sudden interest was not limited to the United States. "You are welcome to stay with us in Holland to see the tulips," one message read. "Thank you for transmitting peace," wrote someone from the Canary Islands. And more: greetings from Ireland, an invitation from Kenya, and a young mother sharing Miss Norma's photos with her ten-month-old baby in Japan. Film crews from France, Korea, and Brazil were begging to embed with our family and follow us on our travels.

Still, I continued to tell myself that all I had to do was stop posting on Miss Norma's Facebook page and then this would all stop and we could return to "normal." It could be that simple, right?

Most afternoons, Tim and I would ride our bikes over the boardwalk and up and down the hard-packed sand of Saint Augustine Beach, trying without success to catch our breath between media requests and hundreds of assorted invitations and heartfelt messages. With the ocean's wind in our faces, and the expansive blue waters offering us some space and clarity, we would use these rides to make decisions to turn down TV talk show requests, continue to find humor in our predicament, and put our relationship above all else.

"How about another lap toward the pier?" Tim said as he raced by me. Maybe if we pedaled fast enough we could leave all of this behind us: our fears of being taken advantage of, of losing our privacy, and of putting Norma in a terrifying situation, plus the deluge of intense emotions coming our way through the Internet.

One evening I picked up a *Reader's Digest* magazine that Norma had recently exchanged one of her action-packed murder-mystery novels for at the RV park's lending library.

Leafing through the tattered periodical, I came across a cartoon of a domestic cat wearing a stocking cap and holding a cup while panhandling on the street. His cardboard sign read FORMER YOUTUBE SENSATION. "That's us," I said in my most reassuring voice. "We're just like the viral cat videos that go around. Eventually the fad comes to an end and things go back to normal."

With apologies to the next person who picked up that magazine, I tore out the page and held on to it as a sign that this too would pass.

But did we really want it to?

In each new message, and in each family conversation about our current situation, I felt a little light turning on inside us.

"I recently lost my father-in-law to cancer. Your story is helping me deal with my grief."

"I am sharing all your posts with the residents in the nursing home where I work. You inspire them to enjoy their last days."

"You are filling a void in the media."

"I am a doctor who will be talking to my patients differently having read your story."

"I was having a horrible day after telling my parents that I am gay. I felt there was no point to living anymore. Then I saw one of your photos and my pain shrank. You chose life, even when that required extraordinary endurance, and now I know I can too."

"You have saved my life. When I see the joy on your face, I know that the best of my life isn't over. You have helped me more than doctors, medicine, or counselors."

"My sister lost her battle today, Miss Norma. I hope you will keep going strong in memory of those who couldn't take your trip with you."

We cried and sometimes laughed over each new message, reading snippets aloud to each other and to Norma, who smiled from ear to ear as she heard stories of people turning their lives around, or we all locked eyes and said a prayer in honor of someone's loss. A wave of love and empathy slowly rolled in to take fear's place in our hearts.

◊ ◊ ◊

In the wake of this shifting in us, we had to make a decision about the CBS interview. Tim was sure that his mom was not made for television. She was timid, always a supporting character in her life—never, ever in the starring role. How could she possibly, at this stage in the game, take a leading role with no practice? No chance.

As Tim and I debated, discussed, and worried over the decision, Norma was deciding all on her own. We do not know what changed with Norma, but to our surprise she began warming up to the idea. "I can do it, Tim," she said to us, certain and steady as ever. Maybe it was her stubbornness. Maybe she just wanted to prove Tim wrong. Maybe, like the balloon ride, she was ready to write another page of her own story. Maybe she had always been a fan of *CBS Evening News*. I do not know for sure, but once she made up her mind, that was it. She wanted to give this thing a try.

Courtney and I came up with a plan: Norma would first have a phone conversation with the CBS producer in Miami, who would be the one to come for the videotaping if things went well. This producer would measure Norma's ability to speak in full sentences without looking to us for reassurance. While

Norma had long been a master of communicating through her body language, her words remained few and far between.

Tim could not handle the thought of his mom embarrassing herself. He took off with Ringo for a walk on the beach, not wanting to witness the disaster that was about to happen when the producer of a nationally broadcast television show heard crickets on the other end of the phone line. With one last look at me—and behind Norma's back—Tim widened his eyes and the edges of his mouth in a look of hopelessness. "I'm out of here. I can't watch this," he said as he closed the motor-home door behind him.

What Tim did not know was that I had been coaching Norma for the past few days when he was not around. We practiced speaking in full sentences, making sure she used more than five words in each one. We practiced not saying "Oh, I don't know" with each question, the answer Tim and I usually got from her no matter what. We had even been having fun with it. Norma and I had a confidence that Tim was unaware of when the phone rang only minutes later.

Hoping my pay-as-you-go cell phone would not run out of minutes, I handed it to Norma. She had used the phone only twice since we had left Michigan.

"Here it goes. It's either sink or swim," I said aloud to no one in particular.

Sitting on the edge of the bed and out of sight, I listened carefully to one end of a pivotal conversation, my hands sweating and my mouth dry with anticipation.

"Oh well, I have never ridden a horse. I think I would like that," she said into the phone. "I have also always wanted to go fly-fishing. That would be neat too."

Yes! That had been more than five words! And her voice had had a strength and conviction I had never heard before.

"Oh sure, we are having a really great time. One of my favorite things was when we went up in the hot-air balloon in Orlando. I can say that I really enjoyed that!"

"She's killing it!" I yell-whispered aloud and rocked back on the bed, my legs and arms pounding the air in utter excitement and pride. I felt like a parent watching her less-than-coordinated child at her first ballet recital; simply not falling down was an accomplishment. Not only was she not falling down; she was practically floating her way through.

When Norma returned the phone to me she had a proud smirk on her face. My heart swelled.

"She did great! No problem. She will be fine," Eliana, the fast-talking producer from Miami said. "We'll be there on Monday and Tuesday. Okay?" It was all now set.

"Well?" Tim asked as he poked his head in the doorway. He seemed hesitant to ask as sweat dripped down his cheeks from jogging back with Ringo—or more likely from nerves.

Norma just smiled. She glanced at me from the corner of her eye and then looked back at Tim. "They are coming out Monday. I must have done okay."

"You're kidding!" Tim exclaimed. "I'm sorry, Mom, but I didn't think you could do it."

"Oh, what are you worried about, Timmy?" Norma asked, reassuring her only son that she really was up for this.

We all had a great laugh and decided it was time to go all in.

Fortunately, correspondent David Begnaud and his production crew were an amazing bunch and helped us settle in to the idea of being viewed on television. By the time the taping of the

CBS piece was finished, and only a week after the GNN story first appeared, the *Driving Miss Norma* Facebook page had 91,000 page "likes." Ninety-one *thousand*!

Norma seemed to enjoy the attention; flattery was not really something she had experienced much of in her life. We surprised ourselves by genuinely enjoying the two-day shoot, and we came away thinking that maybe we could do this and put ourselves out to the world in a big way.

◊ ◊ ◊

Late one evening just a couple of days after the CBS crew had left, we received a photograph on our Facebook page from a sweet-looking gentleman located in Zurich, Switzerland. It showed him holding a handwritten note on a piece of white paper that said "Bravo, Norma, I ♡ you," and we could see that he had signed his name at the bottom. "What a nice man," I said to Tim, sliding the laptop toward him so he could see.

Exhausted, I closed the computer and tried to get some sleep. The next morning when I opened my laptop's silver lid, the photo of the nice man was still up on the screen. Tim and I looked at it more closely and at the same time exclaimed, "Holy shit! That's Paulo Coelho!" The man in the photograph turned out to be the author of *The Alchemist,* a favorite book of mine. He was also the world's most-translated living author and a national hero in his native country of Brazil. Paulo Coelho had posted the photo on his Facebook page too, which happened to have twenty-eight million followers.

The next day the *Driving Miss Norma* page received tens of thousands of messages from around the world, most of them from Brazil. Soon Tim was teaching himself some Portuguese phrases so he could reply to as many of the personal messages from there as possible. The Facebook page received 39,000 new "likes" and we fielded 93 media requests from around the world that day. At one point there were more than 106,000 unread messages, and the computer screen was flashing with new ones coming in faster than we could possibly read them. We had officially gone "viral"—and the CBS piece had not even aired yet.

Nothing else, though, had yet changed in our lives. Norma still followed her routine like clockwork—up at nine in the morning and dancing to bed at nine at night. She would peacefully work on jigsaw puzzles set up on the picnic table outside our motor home, Ringo, her constant companion, napping by her feet while Tim and I went through all the messages. In a virtual sense, everything had changed, but in reality, things were exactly as they had been.

Then one afternoon we took Norma for a walk on Saint Augustine Beach. Tim pushed his mom in her wheelchair over the hard-packed sand while Ringo and I dipped our toes into the water. Two women nearby were out collecting seashells.

"Is that Miss Norma?!" we heard one of the women ask her friend.

"It is—it's her!" the other exclaimed.

Both women quickly approached Norma. "Oh, you are such an inspiration!"

I stood there astonished. The words that I had seen on the computer screen suddenly had breath and faces, gave handshakes and hugs. They smelled of sunscreen and perfume. My tiny mother-in-law had been recognized in public. She was being hailed as a hero.

Sitting tall in her wheelchair, Norma smiled broadly at the women, her eyes full of life. She engaged with these lovely strangers like a professional, laughing and shaking hands.

"It's going to be okay," I whispered to Tim as he positioned himself protectively next to his mom. "She is doing great!"

"I know," he said, before tears flowed down his cheeks. I paused to look at him. I could see now that he was not just protecting her; it was something more. He was proud and touched, overcome by seeing with his own eyes the physical manifestation of Miss Norma's impact on our world.

After that moment, we opened ourselves to embrace everything. I was constantly running out of minutes on my pay-as-you-go phone between countless interviews and long therapeutic phone conversations with my own mom and my best girlfriend, Patti, in Pennsylvania. Reading and replying to messages and sharing stories from former strangers near and far became part of our everyday routine.

In between all of this, Tim, Norma, and I had heart-to-heart-to-heart talks. We were often reminded of the image of a pebble being tossed into the calm waters of a pond and rippling to the edges, the repercussions of which are experienced far beyond the initial location. Only we felt like this was a giant boulder splashing into an ocean, the waves rippling farther than our imagination ever could have taken us.

CHAPTER 10

Kindness

HILTON HEAD ISLAND AND CHARLESTON, SOUTH CAROLINA

MARCH

[Ramie]

Tim and I have known for many years that people are generally kind and caring. Extensive travel has opened our hearts and minds to the beauty and diversity of our country and its people. Over the years we have been on both ends of random acts of kindness, big and small. Giving our umbrella away to a homeless man in a rainstorm or having someone pay for our groceries when we forgot our wallet back at the motor home has become more and more commonplace over the years. We never get tired of it.

As we made our way across the South, we felt those acts of kindness grow unlike anything we had seen before. You might say it was "Southern hospitality"; it felt more to us like we were riding a wave of love across the country.

Invitations rolled in from across the United States and around the world. "Come to California. I will take you tandem paragliding, Miss Norma," read one offer. Another invited us to travel with "A Steampunk Rock-and-Roll Circus" on their tour bus. Ladies-only campouts, free hairdos, and a request for Norma to throw out the first pitch at a Major League Baseball game were all in the mix, along with countless lunch dates and offers to treat her to the best ice cream cones and barbecue in almost every state. If we made our way to Alaska, we were invited to take Miss Norma kayaking, ride in the Iditarod, enjoy a free rental car, and tour the Alaska Marine Highway.

As much as Norma would probably have loved mushing a team of sled dogs, and we certainly would have enjoyed seeing it, we were far from Alaska.

With each accepted invitation, we learned even more how to greet people with open minds and open hearts. When geography and timing allowed us to say "Yes" to a kindness offered, the lines that separate people into different boxes—religion and politics and race and age—blurred and faded and eventually disappeared. Perhaps we experienced something even better than that. We got to see the truth in people, including in Norma: her glow, her tenacity, her joy, and her confidence.

◊ ◊ ◊

In mid-March, we rolled into our new campground on Hilton Head Island, South Carolina. The registration process was predictable, similar to checking into a hotel, with the addition of a short discussion about low branches, sewer hookups, and satellite-dish orientation.

Since traveling with Norma, we were in the habit of grabbing reading material wherever we could get it. Often that meant pulling travel brochures, local newspapers, and a calendar of events off the racks at campground offices. Tim and I would get the motor home parked and hooked up while Norma looked through her new literature. "Well, what looks good, Mom?" Tim always asked. He usually got the same answer every time: "Oh, I don't know. It all looks good." An easy traveler, Norma knew that we would generally come up with a few fun outings at each stop before moving on. She had no agenda. Any excursion was good in her book.

We were in for a surprise on this pleasant Saturday afternoon. "There is a parade tomorrow at three o'clock," she said, "and I would like to go." There was no question in her voice; it was a declarative statement. Miss Norma wanted to go to the parade.

Perhaps she had been emboldened by our experience a couple of days prior when Tim convinced us to accept an invitation to a neighborhood barbecue in Savannah. It had been a going-away party for fellow RVers who had seen our story and were heading out on their own end-of-life journey: they were embarking on a six-month trip with three elderly rescue dogs. Norma had had a burger off the grill and a beer as we regaled the neighborhood with our recent travels. I had watched with pride, hoping she would continue to have the desire to step out of her comfort zone as our journey continued.

Tim was incredulous. "Tomorrow is Sunday, Mom. Are you sure you read that right?"

"Yep. It is right here." She flipped to the page in the *Island Packet* announcing the thirty-third annual Saint Patrick's Day Parade and pointed at the story.

I could tell Tim was hesitating, so I tried to be encouraging. "This is going to be fun! We love parades. Don't we, Timmy?" I said. "Remember when we were in the Baja and seemed to run into parades everywhere we went?"

"But how are we going to find a place to park and get Mom around in her wheelchair in a crowded parade route? I don't know if this is a good idea," Tim countered. He was right about that. We had just arrived on the island and really did not have the lay of the land quite yet. This was not going to be a simple outing.

"Can you try to talk her out of it?" he gently asked me under his breath in a tone her old ears could no longer register.

I must have given Tim a dose of stink eye in response because his affect changed immediately.

"Wait," he said. "I remember getting a message from someone here on Hilton Head not long ago. I didn't respond because we didn't think we were coming this way." Tim began to sort through the thousands of recent messages. "It was a woman with a man's name—Charlie! Here it is! She's with the Chamber of Commerce."

I tried to keep the optimism flowing. "Maybe we can write to her and ask where a good spot to watch the parade in a wheelchair would be."

"It's Saturday. The parade is tomorrow. She won't be answering email now," he said, falling into his old habit of saying "No" before "Yes." "It's too late." Then he added, as if to make it final, "We can't do everything." He had a hundred good reasons not to feel comfortable reaching out to a stranger, but it took only one glance at his mother, playing games on her iPad and still firm in her desire to go, for him to write a note to Charlie.

Leo and Norma
in front of
their house
and gardens
in Presque Isle,
Michigan, in 2011.

Stacy with
Tim at our
wedding
in 2006.

Striking a pose with
the Jolly Green Giant,
Blue Earth, Minnesota.

Pushing the plunger, Mount Rushmore National Memorial, South Dakota.

Toasting to life on the road with Crow Peak beer delivered to our campground in Rapid City, South Dakota.

Learning to trust Tim, Yellowstone National Park.

Giving Ringo a ride, Estes Park, Colorado.

With Penelope the pig, Morgan Stables, Chino Valley, Arizona.

Admiring the Mount Vernon Street
Halloween decorations, Prescott,
Arizona.

With Ringo, Mather Point,
Grand Canyon National Park,
Arizona.

A proud veteran visiting the WWII Museum, New Orleans, Louisiana.

Enjoying lots of Greek food at the Limani, Tarpon Springs, Florida.

On Rick and Jo's boat with Tim, Fort Myers Beach, Florida.

Key Lime Pie! Mucky Duck, Captiva Island, Florida.

Up, up, and away. Our long-awaited hot-air balloon ride, Orlando, Florida.

Glamming it up, Radisson Resort at the Port, Cape Canaveral, Florida.

With Ringo, doing a puzzle outside the RV,
Saint Augustine Beach, Florida.

Relaxing with her buddy,
Savannah, Georgia.

Waving to the crowd, Saint Patrick's Day Parade, Hilton Head Island, South Carolina.

Ramie and Norma sharing a laugh together.

Enjoying the finer things, Belmond Charleston Place, Charleston, South Carolina.

Riding to her birthday party in a 1955 Chevy, Marietta, Georgia.

With Diego at the Georgia Aquarium, Atlanta, Georgia.

Go, Hawks! Atlanta, Georgia.

Sluicing for treasure at the Consolidated Gold Mine, Dahlonega, Georgia.

Miss Norma's first horseback ride, North Carolina Therapeutic Riding Center, Mebane, North Carolina.

Tim letting go of his mom on the zip line, Turtle Run Farm, Graham, North Carolina.

Overlooking the USS Gerald R. Ford, Newport News, Virginia.

Philadelphia freedom! Liberty Bell, Philadelphia, Pennsylvania.

Lobster at Belle Isle Seafood, Winthrop, Massachusetts.

Winthrop police arrive to arrest Miss Norma for excessive cuteness, Winthrop, Massachusetts.

We can do it! Lake George, New York.

Enjoying a Primanti Brothers sandwich and a cold beer in the Strip District, Pittsburgh, Pennsylvania.

Overlooking the skyline, Pittsburgh, Pennsylvania.

Taking a drink from the Zelie Lion, Zelienople, Pennsylvania.

Dodging the water spouts on the Detroit riverfront, Detroit, Michigan.

Living dangerously,
Mammoth Hot Springs,
Yellowstone.

Miss Norma's idea of bliss,
at the Pelindaba Lavender Farm,
Friday Harbor, Washington.

Celebrating 365 days on the road, San Juan Island, Washington.

Laughter and hospice care go nicely with fish and chips at the Bait Shop, Friday Harbor, Washington.

After apologizing for bothering her on a Saturday, Tim wrote, "Miss Norma loves parades, so we will venture out tomorrow afternoon to check it out. If you happen to see this email before-hand, perhaps you can suggest a good spot to view it from. She will be in her wheelchair."

Less than an hour later Charlie responded with parking and parade-viewing recommendations. We began talking about our strategy, how we would leave early enough to find a parking spot and wheel to a nice shady area. As we talked, a *ding* indicated a new email message. Tim looked down at the computer, still sitting squarely on his lap. "Whoa! Now we're talking!" He beamed as he carefully articulated each word of the new email to Norma and me: "Would Miss Norma like to ride *in* the parade? They have an extra car and driver."

We all burst into laughter.

Tim was no longer feeling pessimistic. "What do you think, Mom?!"

"What the heck, why not?!" she said. Then she thought for a minute and added, "Do you think Ringo can go too?"

◊ ◊ ◊

The next morning Charlie picked us up at the campground and provided the four of us with personal limousine service to the dignitaries' luncheon at a local Irish pub. Norma was introduced to all the past grand marshals, a few area mayors, *American Idol* finalist Lee Jean, and a cadre of former strangers who quickly became members of the ever-evolving Miss Norma fan club.

My introverted mother-in-law was named an honorary Hil-ton Head Island Parade Committee member and given a pin and wristband, each affording her special privileges, including free food and drinks before the parade. It was not long before she, Tim, and Ringo were whisked away in an old-fashioned trolley car to the start of the spectacle.

Meanwhile, I was escorted to the dignitaries' grandstand with Lee Jean's mom for the best view of the parade on the island. Next to me sat a large, professional television camera. Across the street was an advertising banner: STREAMING LIVE ON WSAV .COM. As much as I wanted to be in the moment, I also wanted to share this crazy turn of events with someone. Otherwise, I would not have believed it was happening. I sent a quick text message to Patti and her partner April, in Pennsylvania, knowing they would get a kick out of our recent good fortune. Maybe they could see Tim, Norma, and Ringo ride in the parade.

The streets were packed with nearly thirty-five thousand people, all donned in green upon green. High school marching bands, troupes of Irish dancers, fancy cars and floats with local politicians, and elementary school students marched, stepped, and rolled by for hours. A third of the way through the parade I noticed the young teens and preteens in the crowd going wild at the sight of sixteen-year-old Lee Jean in his silver-grey Jaguar convertible. He shyly waved and smiled. His mom leaned toward me and said over the high-pitched screams of the crowd, "He is slowly getting used to his newfound fame."

I had just a moment to ponder the interesting parallels between what these two recently discovered celebrities were experiencing, one a teenager and the other a nonagenarian, and then I saw it: the next car behind the sporty Jaguar was a kelly-green Ford Mustang convertible. The crowd's youthful energy dissipated and a decidedly older set were alert to its passengers. The side panel of this next car read MISS NORMA.

My bird's-eye view allowed me to see the length of Pope Avenue. The trees were starting to wake up from their winter's rest with delicate buds, decorating the island just in time for the Irish-inspired spectacle. As the Mustang crept closer, I chuckled as I caught sight of Ringo in the front seat. Then I saw something that took my breath away: an almost unrecognizable smile on Norma's face. Sitting high atop the backseat, she waved and smiled like she had just won a homecoming queen crown. She seemed more alive than ever before and positively glowed up there. She did not seem to have a bashful or shy bone in her body in that moment.

I could not contain my pride and joy. I got to my feet and waved back at her along with the rest of the crowd. I clapped and swayed a little to the music of a marching band I could hear coming up behind them. Like the teenage girls just minutes before, I yelped in adoration, swept up in feeling. Here she was, living large, embracing her newfound celebrity status with open, waving arms, and her infectious smile was carrying the throngs of people on the parade route along with her.

My cell phone vibrated in my camera bag. A text from Patti read, "We just saw them! We just saw them! OMG! U guys R LIVING!" The next message read, "Did you get to meet Lee Jean? WE LOVE HIM!" I laughed, delighted that I could share the moment with someone.

As the rest of the parade flowed by me, with adrenaline still pumping through my veins, I found myself thinking of the last time I had seen Norma in a hot rod like that. About fifteen years ago Stacy had gifted Leo with a 1988 supercharged Toyota

MR2, or, as the family liked to call it, Mister 2. There were very few imported to the States—and even fewer of them left now, since they are speedy little cars and speedy drivers have turned them mostly into piles of twisted metal. Speed had not mattered to Leo and Norma. They were entering their eighties and knew better than to wrap this go-cart around a tree. They would head to church with the T-top panels off and the wind blowing in their hair. It had been their "Sunday drive" car, and Norma had many fond memories of Leo spinning the tires on the gravel country roads of northern Michigan with her riding shotgun in the grey two-seater. Earlier that morning Norma had told me that she had only ever been in one other parade. "It was in Dad's sports car, Mister 2," she shared. "You know, just two laps around the Presque Isle lighthouse and in ten minutes the whole parade is over."

If only Leo could see her now, I thought, as she commanded the attention of thousands of people.

That night at nine o'clock we sang and danced to bed as usual, this time to the beat of a marching band, Norma using her cane as a majorette baton.

"How are you feeling after that amazing day, Norma?" I was hoping for a thoughtful response about how extraordinary it was to have all those people cheer for her, or maybe a comment about the beautiful floats she had seen from the grandstand after she made it through the route, or that she was now invited to do more cool things around the area, like meet the Budweiser Clydesdales and go to an exclusive private beach.

"I don't know what to say," Norma reflected, "but I'll tell you one thing." She paused, as if she had practiced perfect comedic timing, and then said, "My arm sure is going to be sore tomorrow! That was a lot of waving."

◊ ◊ ◊

The following week, our new friend Charlie helped arrange for us to travel two hours north of Hilton Head Island to visit historic Charleston, South Carolina. We ended up with reservations at the city's nicest hotel, Belmond Charleston Place, for the duration of our visit. The hotel was just steps from lots of attractions, so we could take Norma to see all sorts of places with the added support of her wheelchair.

We arrived before check-in time and were surprised and overcome with gratitude to find that our rooms had been upgraded to "Club Level," which included complimentary food and beverages served five times each day. The hotel also waived its customary pet fee for Ringo.

"How about a glass of champagne, Mom," Tim asked Norma as we sat in the lounge waiting for our rooms to be readied. We had realized earlier that morning, as we loaded the Jeep, that our Charleston trip coincided with Leo's birthday. We wanted to try to make it a special day.

"Sure. Why not?" she responded.

Tim headed up the large, winding stairs to the bar and dining area while Norma, Ringo, and I waited in the lower lounge, where we had to hang out because Ringo could not be near the food buffets. When Tim came back, he had fancy flutes of champagne as well as two young bartenders named Amanda and Robin in tow. "They wanted to come and meet you, Mom," he said as he introduced them to Norma.

To me he said, "I told them my mom's story while they poured our champagne, and they were excited to meet her. I warned them that she might be a little melancholy today because it's Dad's birthday—the first since he died."

After a few minutes of greetings and chatting it was time for our new friends to get back to work, but before they started on their way up to the bar, they implored us to stop by for dinner and cocktails later that evening.

"We would love to," I responded.

Right after Amanda and Robin left, a large man appeared with an envelope. "Are you Miss Norma?" he asked.

Norma's slight frame was just beginning to make a dent in the tight black leather couch where she sat, the glass of champagne held in her boney left hand. Leaning forward slightly, she said, "I am Norma." She looked up at the slightly daunting figure now standing next to her. His eyes were kind, and Norma's sweet smile followed shortly.

"My name is Gary. I'm with the Convention and Visitors Bureau. We are thrilled that you are in our city."

"It is nice to be here," Norma easily replied.

"I have a welcome gift for you," he continued. "We would like you to enjoy our city. Here are VIP tickets to any and all attractions in Charleston and the surrounding area, including historic home tours, carriage rides, plantations and gardens, harbor tours—you name it!"

Norma was wide-eyed and all ears.

"There is only one catch . . ."

I glanced nervously from Norma to Tim. What could this catch be? By accepting this generosity have we walked into something bad? Are we being used? Warning signals were flashing red in my mind, always thinking first of how to protect my family. I could tell Tim was having the same concerns.

But Gary only said, "Can I have a hug, Miss Norma?" He told us that he had lost his mom, and he really missed her. Using us for promotions or whatever other awful requests my mind had conjured up were the furthest things from his intentions. "It would make me very happy if you didn't even open your computer while you're here," he told us. "Please, enjoy yourselves."

And so Gary got his hug, and we got an all-access pass to the wonderful art and culture of Charleston. Much more important, though, we got a lesson in staying openhearted.

We settled into our rooms after that and rested awhile until it was time for dinner. While Ringo enjoyed the thousand-thread-count sheets on the king-size bed in the Presidential Suite, we headed to the bar and restaurant.

I had never known my mother-in-law as much of a drinker. It seemed as though on this trip she had decided she enjoyed a beer with Tim at the end of each day. Cocktails had certainly never been her thing. But as a child of the Great Depression, anything that was free caught her attention.

"What will it be, Miss Norma?" said Amanda, winning her over with her natural charm and hospitality.

A fish out of water, Norma looked to Tim for a response. She was up for the new adventure; she just did not know what to order.

"Have you ever had a gin and tonic, Mom?"

"No, I don't imagine I have," she replied.

"Let's start there, Amanda," Tim said to our new friend.

The gourmet food seemed endless, and the drinks Amanda poured became more and more exotic as the evening went on. In truth, everything was exotic to Norma, and she now found out that everyone had a unique story to tell. We learned that Amanda's passion was not slinging drinks but composing music, and she hoped to someday create a movie score.

Ten o'clock was last call at the Club Level bar, and we were all having so much fun Norma barely noticed that her bedtime had come and gone. Most everyone had left by now, either back to their rooms or to one of the hotel's other public bars. We were nursing what was left of our drinks, sitting at the bar, and still talking with Amanda and Robin.

When we were just about ready to call it a night and return to our rooms, Robin went into the back and returned with a plate, beaming as she placed it before us. On it was a small chocolate rum cake accented with sour cherries, whipped cream, and two glowing candles. "Happy Birthday, Leo" was piped in chocolate icing on the plate.

I caught my breath and put my hand to my mouth. The burning candles lit up Norma's face and glowed even brighter in their reflection in her glasses. It was so sudden, so unexpected, and so thoughtful that we were all instantly brought to tears, even the two hotel employees. Overcome, the three of us leaned in, puffed up our chests, and blew out the candles.

It had been nearly nine months since Leo's death and we had been so busy, had gone through so many changes, we had hardly looked back. This simple gesture allowed us to stop for a moment to remember and mourn our loss.

Later that night, fresh tears in his eyes, Tim whispered to me, "That was the first time I have ever seen my mom cry over my dad's death. What a gift."

CHAPTER 11

Celebration

MARIETTA AND ATLANTA, GEORGIA

MARCH

[Tim]

By the time we crossed the border into Georgia, we had all stopped resisting and began to embrace the new experiences that continually came our way. So when a woman from Marietta, Georgia, who had been following our Facebook page, invited us to have lunch with her in the courtyard of her B and B in Savannah, we said "Yes."

Toren instantly fell in love with my mom. When we told her that Mom's ninety-first birthday was coming up on March 31, she invited us to stay with her and her teenage son, Aidan, at their home and to celebrate Mom's birthday at Marietta Square. Toren said that she wanted it to be a very special day for Miss Norma, and she was determined to get her whole community involved in the celebration.

Ramie and I did not have anything in particular in mind to commemorate Mom's birthday. At best, we hoped we could arrange it so that we were not celebrating the occasion alone in a parking lot somewhere on the road. We asked Mom what she thought of spending her birthday with Toren and Aidan in Marietta.

"Sure, I guess so," she replied, with only a hint of hesitation.

The motor home needed some maintenance, so we arrived a day early, leaving it at a nearby RV repair shop. We each packed a small bag of clothes and toiletries, and then drove the Jeep to Toren's house, where we would spend the next five days. Despite her initial approval, Mom seemed uncomfortable about the situation after we got there. When she hesitated to use the guest-room shower that night, I had to ask her what was going on.

"I have never used someone else's shower before," she said, slightly embarrassed.

I reflected on the fact that my parents had rarely traveled in their married life, and most certainly had never spent the night in a stranger's house.

The following morning we parked the Jeep in a lot a few blocks from Marietta Square, where Toren had said there would be someone waiting for us. We saw a red-and-white '55 Chevy idling nearby with a pair of fuzzy dice hanging from the rear-view mirror, the blue smoke from its exhaust indicating that the old engine was burning a little oil. "This must be our ride," I said to my passengers.

With a flourish, Lenny, our driver, opened the Chevy's rear door and helped Mom into the backseat, careful not to knock the birthday tiara Toren earlier had placed on her head against the car's bright red velour headliner. By the time he had closed the door, however, the car had stalled out. Frantically pumping the gas pedal while turning the ignition key, he was rewarded with only a bang and a few small puffs of smoke. The engine finally fired and we were propelled forward, only to stall again at an intersection, a mere city block from our destination.

"Should we offer to get out and push?" I whispered to Ramie, who was sitting next to me in the backseat. "If we can make this turn, it's all downhill to the Square."

Ramie liked the idea, but before we could act on my plan, the car erupted back to life. As we turned down the street, we could see ahead that there was a lot of commotion in front of the Marietta Local, the popular restaurant that was hosting us. A police cruiser and a fire truck were parked at the curb, and blue-clad personnel stood on the sidewalk, along with hundreds of excited well-wishers. Purple, pink, and green balloon bouquets overflowed into the street. Two Atlanta Hawks cheerleaders were near the door, shaking their pom-poms. And a large group of media types were at the curb, brandishing cameras, microphones, and notepads.

"What have we gotten ourselves into?" I murmured. In front of us was a spectacle that I had never really expected to see, and I was afraid this event was going to be too over-the-top for all of us. We barely got Mom out of the car and into her wheelchair before being mobbed by the friendly crowd. All Ramie and I could do was back off and hope that Miss Norma could handle the crush of attention. We both were a little surprised when we saw that she certainly could hold her own.

Here was my mom, a humble, quiet woman who had never imposed on anyone in her life. She and Dad had generally observed their birthdays by eating an early dinner at an Applebee's restaurant in Alpena, Michigan, twenty-five miles from their Presque Isle home. Ramie and I would call from wherever we were to sing "Happy Birthday" and to hear what they had eaten. Birthdays had never really been a big deal in our family. "You're just another year older, that's all," my dad would say. Mom would bake a cake for my sister and me, but we never had the classic birthday celebration with a bunch of other children over for a party like many of our peers did.

Because she always declined attention and praise, Mom had much more often been the one giving, not receiving, love and care. She had lived to see ninety-one, and she had done so by choosing to spend her final days, however long they might be, on an adventure on her own terms. And the entire city of Marietta, it seemed, was not going to let her get away with refusing to celebrate herself. People of all ages were clamoring to get a photo with Mom, to wish her "Happy Birthday," or just to be near her. I was standing several feet away, almost in the street, talking to Jim, the owner of the Marietta Local.

"I hear that you like to cook, Tim," he said as we continued to watch the action on the corner. "I have something very special in mind for you this morning. How would you like to cook our signature breakfast dish for your mama's birthday?"

How could I say no to his kind offer?

He presented me with a black chef's jacket and an apron as he introduced me to his executive chef, Briton, who led me into the restaurant's professional kitchen to make french toast and spicy fried chicken. Following her lead, I donned latex gloves and dipped thick-sliced brioche into the prepared egg batter. After placing the soggy bread on the flattop griddle to cook, I turned my attention to battering the chicken breasts, eventually dropping them into the deep fryer to cook until reaching a golden brown. Everything properly prepared, I plated our dishes and topped off the french toast with some warm apple compote before dusting it with powdered sugar. I grabbed the plates and hurriedly returned to the dining room. I had gone from being apprehensive about the size of the party to being afraid that I was missing out. I wanted to be part of the celebration.

The party was indeed in full swing by now, and this was my first chance to take in the whole scene. Large gold balloon letters spelled out NORMA IS 91 across the long, exposed-brick wall that dominated the space. Every table overflowed with floral bouquets and decorations. Several small-scale hot-air balloons, complete with tiny passenger baskets, floated around the room as a nod to Mom's balloon ride a little more than two months before. Two guys were picking bluegrass on a banjo and a guitar in the corner, creating the perfect musical background for the affair. And the whole place was packed with celebrants who all made their way down the "biscuit bar" that Jim and his wife, Sophia, had set up that morning. It was incredibly festive.

Mom had just finished having her photograph taken with the two visiting Hawks cheerleaders, who I could see were fawning over her. They gave her a "swag bag" filled with all kinds of NBA-logo merchandise, including a signed jersey from forward Mike Muscala, his number 31 a homage to Mom's birth date. Also included were three tickets to see the Hawks play the Cleveland Cavaliers the following night. It was a bit overwhelming for all of us.

"Look at this, Timmy," Mom said as she sat down to eat my breakfast creation. On her wrist was a beautiful silver bracelet laden with charms that represented her journey so far: a hot-air balloon, an outline of the state of Georgia, a seashell, and the numeral 91. "A local jewelry store owner gave this to me," she added. I could see that many of the Square's business owners had given her gift baskets or items from their shops, and they were piled up beside her on the table. Mom had never received so many gifts at one time in her entire life.

Finally it was time for the birthday cake. Creating a new Southern tradition, Jim had made a giant biscuit nearly the size of a manhole cover, set it on an elevated cake tray, and studded it with birthday candles. "Sorry, there's not enough room for ninety-one lit candles here," he said with a laugh. Still, the large number was daunting enough for someone with such small lungs to blow them out. Mom had nothing to fear, though, because three attendant Marietta city firemen quickly rushed to her side to help with the task.

"What's your birthday wish, Miss Norma?" someone shouted.

Mom paused and reflected a few moments before answering. "That I live to see ninety-two," she finally said.

◊ ◊ ◊

Mom continued to celebrate her birthday the following day in Atlanta. The Hawks basketball organization contacted us to see what hotel we were registered at. "We would like to send a limousine to take you to the game," they said. Explaining that we were staying with a woman we had just met through Facebook, at her home in Marietta, they indicated that would not do. "We would like you all to be our guests at the Omni Atlanta Hotel," they continued. "Then you won't have to take Miss Norma outside to go to the basketball game."

None of us was sure what that meant, but we were happy to accept their offer nonetheless. It would be a real treat to stay in a hotel again. We had a big day planned in Atlanta. Not only were we going to see the basketball game that night, but we had also accepted an invitation to visit the Georgia Aquarium, the largest in the Western Hemisphere.

I rolled Mom past giant marble pillars and into the lobby of the luxury high-rise hotel feeling a little self-conscious. We were traveling the country together in a motor home and there-fore had little use for formal luggage. Draped on the handles of her wheelchair were assorted beach bags containing our clothes and toiletries. Ramie followed close behind clutching coats, a purse, and her camera bag. "Oh my, we look just like the Bev-erly Hillbillies," Mom said to me, referring to the 1960s sitcom I had watched as a child.

Before we could retreat, Leslie, the hotel manager, spotted us. "Why, welcome and Happy Birthday, Miss Norma," she said with a Southern drawl and a genuine smile. Camera flashes went off as some of the assembled front-desk staff crowned Mom with yet another tiara and draped a birthday sash across her chest.

We were shown to our adjoining rooms on the tenth floor with balconies overlooking the lively CNN Center atrium below. As I stood next to Mom, we watched people ride an eight-story es-calator up to a giant Earth globe, which was the staging area for the news network's studio tour. I pointed to the windows where we could see journalists working, some broadcasting live. "Do you suppose Anderson Cooper can see us?" Mom asked when she realized Gloria Vanderbilt's son could be one of them.

We did not have time to savor the view, however, since we both heard a knock on the door. It was room service delivering a chocolate cake and a bucket of iced-down beers, compliments of the hotel. Ramie had posted a picture of Mom at a party with five kinds of cake in front of her and making a face while drink-ing a beer, and we seem to have started a trend. Everywhere we went we were inundated with cake and beer. In fact, this was our third cake since leaving the party in Marietta the day before. It was all delicious and extremely generous of everyone, but the three of us had pretty much had our fill of sweets. "Why couldn't I have said that I liked cheese and crackers instead?" Mom laughed as we all looked at our waistlines.

The hotel limousine delivered us to the Georgia Aquarium's front entrance just in time for our one o'clock appointment. Ramie and I were particularly excited to show Mom the Ocean Voyager exhibit with its four whale sharks, the only captive ones outside of Asia. We had already told her about the whale sharks that frequented the Baja California bay where we hoped to take her, and we wanted her to get an idea of what the largest fishes in the world looked like.

Greeted by four staff members, we were brought through the crowded main entrance. The staff motioned everyone to the side to make way for Mom's wheelchair, parting the mass of people like Moses did the Red Sea. We did not have to struggle with the throngs for long since we were soon diverted into an un-marked hallway behind a locked door.

"We have some special things planned for you today, Miss Norma," Megan, the aquarium's public relations coordinator said as she led the way. "Let's go into this room first and meet Diego."

Diego, we soon found out, was the aquarium's star-attraction sea lion, and we found him relaxing in his inner sanctum. The long and somewhat narrow room contained a large pool with simulated rock features running the full length of the back. The tank, fronted by three inches of acrylic, was about four feet high yet low enough for Diego to hang over the edge, which is how we found him when we entered.

Little had Mom known that she would spend the next twenty minutes hanging out with one of the most adorable characters she had met on her adventure so far. She was invited to touch the sea lion and note the different textures of his skin and fur. Mom and Diego stuck their tongues out at each other, posed for photographs, and enjoyed a mock kiss before it was time to move on. "That sea lion had really bad breath," Mom whispered into my ear as I wheeled her out the door.

Our aquarium guides continued to lead us through a labyrinth of hallways and explained the inner workings of the three-hundred-million-dollar facility. We went by the state-of-the-art diagnostic laboratory and veterinary hospital, equipped to handle even a sick whale shark. Next was the husbandry commissary, a specially designed kitchen that is held to higher standards than restaurant kitchens and prepares all the food for the tens of thousands of fish and animals.

Soon we exited the corridor and entered what appeared to be a ballroom. Mom just gasped at what she saw when I pushed her wheelchair around the corner. In front of us was a ten-foot-high wall of acrylic that ran the entire length of the room and separated us from the backside of the Ocean Explorer exhibit. The aquarium's chief operating officer, Joe, and some of the staff were waiting to fête Mom with a little party. There was more cake and beer—this time, a whale-shark-themed cake and a whole bucket of assorted beers—and we sat and enjoyed the comestibles with Joe while we were hypnotized by the aquatic splendor before us.

Fortified with the cake and beer, we had to wind up our tour to return to the hotel in time for the basketball game. We could not resist seeing the four resident beluga whales before leaving, however, and Mom had to cover her ears when the adorable animals made high-pitched noises from the nasal sacs near their blowholes.

◊ ◊ ◊

The game that night was the hottest ticket in town. "King James" himself, Cleveland Cavaliers star LeBron James, was playing, and that always meant a sell-out crowd.

But no one could have found a more ardent or dapper Atlanta Hawks fan than my mom that evening. Her lime-green shirt highlighted the reds and greens of the fan jersey she wore over it, and the oversize Hawks ball cap, cocked at a slight angle on her head, made it look like she was straight out of a hip-hop music video. In her lap were assorted noisemakers and a large foam hand that said GO HAWKS. As we waited for our hosts, many basketball fans stopped by to take selfies with Mom. We could not understand the sudden burst of interest until one guy said, "The Hawks just put out a social-media blast on Twitter and Instagram about you guys."

A side door near the main entrance opened, and the two cheerleaders who had been at Mom's birthday party the day before came out, intending to entertain the fans waiting in line. They saw us first and immediately ran our way, crouching down to talk to Mom in her wheelchair when they reached her. "You look so cute tonight, Miss Norma," they said as they handed me their phones to take photographs. I could see that many of the people in line were now wondering why this old lady was capturing so much attention.

Soon the door opened again, and Margo, the Hawks corporate social responsibility coordinator, waved us into the arena. "We are so happy to have you here for the game," she said enthusiastically as she ushered us through security. "We have several surprises for you this evening."

Mom had never been in a modern sports arena, and even Ramie and I were a little taken aback by the size and grandeur of Philips Arena. "Just look at this place," Mom murmured in awe as I pushed her wheelchair through the crowded outer area.

We followed Margo and her assistant to the arena's upper-level deck, where there was a wide row of single chairs instead of fixed seats. "This is going to be great," I said to Mom as I looked at our unobstructed view of the court below.

But we did not stay put for long—we were quickly ushered back down to the lower level and through a tunnel that led to the floor. Signing autographs courtside was NBA Hall of Famer Dominique Wilkins. The six-foot-eight former-Hawks star player was known as one of the league's best slam-dunkers, and he towered over us all as we were photographed with him. We were then invited to sit in some front-row seats to hang out for a bit, and we marveled at how comfortable they were compared to regular arena seating.

When he was finished with his fans, Dominique came over and sat down next to my mom. He gave her a big kiss on the cheek and placed his arm around her. They began talking, but I was unable to hear their conversation, only Mom's laughs. To me, she was obviously charmed by this man in a suit wearing size-15 shoes.

The Hawks head coach soon approached and said, "I hear that Miss Norma is going to be my co-captain for the game tonight. You and your wife will probably have to help her get to center court."

Easing Mom out of her wheelchair, Ramie and I each took one of her arms and walked her onto the floor to participate in the referee meeting with the captains of the Hawks and the Cavaliers. "I can't believe all of this," Mom said to me as we gazed at the nearly twenty thousand spectators looking down at us.

Anxious now to get to our seats and watch the game, we followed our guides back to the entrance tunnel.

"Miss Norma, Miss Norma, wait!" we heard someone yelling from nearby. "I want to talk to you." We all looked up to see a young man in his twenties bounding through the crowd and heading our way. Catching up to us he added, "My name is Oliver, and my dad owns the team."

The looks on our handlers' faces revealed that he was indeed the son of the man who had recently bought the Hawks.

"I just want to thank you for being an inspiration to my family," he continued. "After reading about your story, we took our first family vacation together, ever. It was great!" He leaned over and gave my mom a big hug.

She just smiled. I knew Mom was already having a tough time grasping the idea that she was somehow inspiring people from all over the world and from all walks of life. Now she had just heard she had inspired a billionaire and his actress wife to take their children somewhere to share family time. Even Ramie and I were having a hard time believing her story could be this powerful.

We returned to our seats just as a laser-light show illuminated the court to introduce the Hawks starting lineup. The Cavaliers were on a winning streak and were heavily favored to win. Near the end of the first half, they were ahead 41–28.

During a time-out just before halftime, my mom's face suddenly appeared on the jumbotron screen that dominated the space above center court. I could tell something was going to happen when the entire Atlanta Hawks cheerleading squad suddenly appeared and surrounded her wheelchair. A cameraman showed up several minutes later, and the next thing we knew, Mom was waving and shaking pom-poms for thirty seconds with women nearly seven decades her junior.

The Hawks made a comeback in the second half, eventually tying the score with a three-pointer at the buzzer, forcing the game into overtime. It was already hours after Mom's usual bedtime, but I could see that she was still wide awake as she continued to cheer and wave her red towel with every Hawks score. Ramie and I just looked at each other, truly impressed by her stamina.

Our new favorite team lost that night—barely. We wheeled Mom through the crowd and straight back to our adjoining hotel, carrying yet another cake, which the Hawks had given us at the game. We all had to agree that none of us had ever had a birthday celebration quite as exciting as this one, or had ever eaten this much cake in one day.

CHAPTER 12

Integrity

NEWPORT NEWS. VIRGINIA

APRIL

[Tim]

With over six years difference between us, Stacy and I had been far enough apart in age that we did not do a lot together, with one exception. We loved to play what we simply called "Spy!" With the secret-agent kit that had been sent to me in return for a slew of cereal box tops, we used a periscope-type device to look around corners without being seen and set trip wires in the hallway to alert us of our parents' imminent arrival. "Spying" on Mom and Dad, and even the family dog, had been a regular weekend activity for my sister and me in the late 1960s. When Stacy grew up to become a high-ranking special agent in the United States Secret Service, I teased that her successful career was all thanks to our childhood shenanigans.

One day, early in her career, Stacy found herself assigned to protect former president Gerald R. Ford. After that assignment, a story I had heard my whole life from my parents became one I would hear from my sister too. As Stacy told it, she introduced herself to the "accidental" president while riding in his armored limousine.

"Mister President," she said with confidence, "I'm Special Agent Stacy Bauerschmidt. You may not remember, but you helped my parents out many years ago after World War Two."

A veteran of that war himself, Ford thought aloud in response, "Bauerschmidt, Bauerschmidt." He sat for a moment behind the limousine's bulletproof windows and then matter-of-factly said, "I do remember your parents." He went on to retell the story Stacy and I had heard many times before.

It was 1949. Mom and Dad were back from the war, recently married, and living in a fifteen-foot travel trailer without a bathroom. The GI Bill provided money to veterans wishing to go back to school. Mom wanted to be an artist and Dad wanted to become a watchmaker, so they decided to temporarily move from their hometown of Toledo to Grand Rapids, Michigan, so that Mom could attend Kendall College of Art and Design.

Towing their home behind their dark blue 1940 Ford sedan, they parked in a motor court and began their studies. But soon money became scarce, since their veterans' checks had not caught up with them in the move. Sitting at their tiny drop-leaf table in the trailer, they emptied their pockets of all the money they had in the world and pushed it to the center. It amounted to three pennies. "This won't even buy a loaf of bread," Mom said. "We have to do something. What should we do?"

Then she got an idea. Pulling out her best stationery, she penned a letter, explaining their situation, to Gerald Ford, their young congressman from Michigan's Fifth Congressional District, who had been elected only months before. During his 1948 campaign, Ford had visited voters on their doorsteps and had met them as they left their jobs at the factories. He was known for being very connected with his constituency.

Dad was pessimistic, but he did not have a better idea. He murmured "Let's see if this new guy is all he is cracked up to be" as he took Mom's handwritten letter to the mailbox. They spent their last three cents on the stamp.

About ten days later, Mom and Dad heard a knock on their trailer door. "Hello?" Mom said as she opened it. There in the motor court stood Congressman Ford himself, delivering their overdue checks personally. Now they could begin the lives they had dreamed of.

In Stacy's line of work, she could not afford to be starstruck. She just could not. But the day President Ford repeated the story she had heard many times before from our parents, she became an admirer of his. Over time, her relationship with the Ford family grew, and when, in 2006, the former president was at the end of his life, Stacy was there with the family and helped them to make decisions. One of her Secret Service responsibilities had been to oversee the planning of state funerals, and so she had the honor of offering this man, who had meant so much to her parents, a final thank-you.

◊ ◊ ◊

My parents were like plenty of others of their generation who had served, doing their duty and returning home but not feeling like the work they had done mattered much. In the Army Air Corp, Dad had worked in the office "shuffling papers," he had said. When Mom was a nurse with the WAVES at the San Diego Naval Hospital, she had mostly cared for officers and their wives, administering hundreds of penicillin shots over her short time in the service. They had both downplayed their roles in the war since they had never been in combat like so many of their peers. Most who knew Mom and Dad over the years, even their closest friends, never found out they had served. "It just didn't come up," Mom told us later.

Our stop in New Orleans, Louisiana, to spend the previous Thanksgiving holiday had changed all that. Not only is the "Big Easy" the home of the Mardi Gras, great food, and lively music, but the National WWII Museum is also an attraction. We had read good things about the museum, and Mom was excited to go. The morning we rolled her into the lobby, there were very few people visiting. The young woman at the ticket counter asked if Mom was a World War II veteran.

Mom sheepishly said, "Yes, I suppose I am."

"Well, then there is no charge for you, ma'am," the ticket agent excitedly announced.

Mom straightened up in her wheelchair and accepted that free admission with pride and gratitude. She was then given a large red, white, and blue laminated tag on a lanyard indicating that she was a World War II veteran.

The staff went wild when they learned she had been in the WAVES. "It is really rare that we get to meet one of the WAVES," we were told as we greeted several museum employees. Word got out, and as we made our way through the museum, we overheard excited voices. "See that woman over there in the wheelchair? She was in the WAVES! I can't believe it!" and "Wow, what an honor! We hardly ever get WAVES here!"

The museum was designed to give the visitor a sense of what it was like for people like my mom, Dad, Uncle Ralph, and sixteen million other young Americans to go off to war. After we were all issued mock dog tags, we boarded a stationary rail car that used vintage film footage projected onto the windows to simulate a troop transport to a basic training camp. Mom could not keep the memories from flooding back. She recalled her few months of basic training at Hunter College in New York before she traveled west by train to San Diego. We could almost see her reliving the experience.

It was fun to see her change from someone who had downplayed her service all her life into someone who was celebrated for it. Several people saw the Facebook post of our museum visit and wrote to extend their gratitude to Mom also.

One message happened to be from a former student of Ramie's from her days as a middle school counselor. Ramie knew Elise, now in her early twenties and a navy petty officer, as a bright, caring, and mature young lady. Elise thanked Mom for paving a path for women like her to be able to serve their country. She also said, "If your travels ever bring you to the East Coast, please let me know. Maybe we can do something special for Miss Norma on the USS *Gerald R. Ford*."

When Ramie read the message aloud, Mom's eyebrows shot up to her hairline. It was clear that this was an invitation to pay attention to. Then it dawned on us: Elise did not know President Ford's connection to our family, and she might enjoy hearing the story. Ramie sent her the abridged version, but at that time, we had no idea what our travel plans would be after wintering in Florida. So we just thanked Elise for her thoughtfulness and told her we would let her know our decision about visiting once our travel plans became clearer.

Not long after that we were contacted by the ship's public relations officer, the shipbuilder's marketing coordinator, and eventually the commanding officer himself. They each hoped to get us on board the USS *Gerald R. Ford* for its formal dedication in early April.

"That would be really great," Mom said. So Ramie and I began to organize our travel plans around a stop in Newport News, Virginia, to coincide with the event.

Ramie let Elise know, and Elise replied that everyone was excited to have us there. In her email she said, "All we need are copies of your passports or birth certificates so we can put you through a security clearance. Once that happens, we can get you on the ship, no problem."

My heart sank. When leaving Michigan, Ramie and I had never imagined taking Mom out of the country on this adventure. Her almost-expired passport was locked away in a safety deposit box in northern Michigan, and there was no way for us to get it. We were crestfallen.

We replied with the bad news and it took a few weeks to hear back from Elise and the others. This security issue was clearly getting in the way of our visit. Then it dawned on us that maybe the solution was simple. The whole Bauerschmidt family had been vetted by the United States Secret Service when Stacy had become an agent, and there certainly must be some record of Mom being an upstanding citizen. We told both the navy and the Newport News shipbuilders that all they had to do was call the Secret Service and everyone there would tell them that Norma Bauerschmidt was not a ninety-one-year-old spy.

We did not hear back from either of them. Nor did we receive clearance in time for the formal dedication ceremony. We were in North Carolina when a call came in one morning, though, from the outgoing commanding officer of the ship, who apparently was anxious to have Mom at the dedication ceremony in spirit at least.

Mom was nervous and extremely excited that Captain Meier wanted to talk with her, "of all people," she said. She sat up straight in the dinette when Ramie passed her the cell phone. I listened as she talked to the captain and then told him the same story my sister and I had always heard when we were growing up. After she finished, she said, "Gerald Ford was a man of integrity. He was a good man."

Mom and Dad's chance encounter with freshman congressman Ford was the foundation of Captain Meier's speech an hour later, when he dedicated a statue depicting Ford as a young naval officer. The statue is the centerpiece of a memorial located at the helm of the most technologically advanced aircraft carrier in the world, and it will serve for many years to come as a constant reminder of maintaining "integrity at the helm."

A few weeks later, we were finally cleared to board the ship. No reason was given. It was evident to us what had happened, though: Stacy always seemed to have a hand in making our impossible situations possible.

◊ ◊ ◊

On the day of our visit to the USS *Gerald R. Ford* it was mild enough for us all to leave our jackets at home. We made sure to leave our campground in Suffolk, Virginia, early enough to get to the shipbuilder's office in time to check in before our one o'clock scheduled tour. As we crossed the bridge spanning the

James River, we could see several ships being built or overhauled at the Newport News shipyard. One stood out by its sheer size. Rising nearly two hundred fifty feet above the waterline and at over eleven hundred feet long, the thirteen-billion-dollar carrier dominated the horizon.

We arrived at the headquarters of Huntington Ingalls Industries to find a parking spot near the entrance with a sign that said RESERVED FOR MISS NORMA. I stayed with Mom as Ramie went in to meet Christie, our contact with the company, and to present her with our identifications.

"We have to wait here for their security guy to show up," Ramie related to Mom and me when she returned. "He is the one that will be driving us to the shipyard."

Soon an unassuming white minivan arrived and pulled up behind the Jeep. A middle-aged man wearing Ray-Ban Wayfarer sunglasses emerged to greet us. "Hi. I'm Gerry, director of security for the shipbuilder," he said. "I'll be your escort for the day."

While Ramie and Mom were trying on the hard hats and safety glasses Gerry said we needed for our visit, he surprised me with something very personal. "I knew your sister, Stacy," he said to me in a low voice. "I worked with her for many years in DC with the Secret Service."

I had been out of touch with Stacy's friends in the Service since her death. Here I had a chance to talk again with someone who had actually worked with her, and I was eager to find out how well he really knew her.

"Stacy would come down and stay with my family after I retired down here. I would always have to ask her to watch her language when my two little ones were around." He chuckled.

Yes, he had known Stacy pretty well, all right.

With security passes clipped to our shirts, we all loaded into the minivan and drove to the historic shipyard, a short distance away. Founded as the Chesapeake Dry Dock and Construction Company in 1886, Newport News Shipbuilding has since constructed more than eight hundred naval and commercial vessels. The company now not only builds and refurbishes ships for the navy but fabricates Virginia-class nuclear submarines for it as well.

Gerry drove us along one side of the five-hundred-fifty-acre shipyard before turning into one of the many entrance gates. He had to time our arrival perfectly, because the secure facility was shut down to vehicles during shift changes due to the great number of workers walking around. The armed guard at the gate nodded in approval at our passes and we gained access. We drove past a hodgepodge of old industrial buildings and dodged forklifts laden with matériel before the waterfront finally came into view.

Knowing that my mom had limited mobility, our hosts had made accommodations for her visit. Typically, ship workers, navy personnel, and others boarded the vessel by foot. When we arrived, however, Gerry made a beeline for a long ramp that led straight up into the hangar deck of the ship, which was large enough to hold seventy-five aircraft.

We were greeted by a horde of still and video photographers when the minivan halted inside. We meekly waved at the assembled crowd. The carrier was just beginning to be commissioned by the navy, so there was a mix of civilian shipbuilders and about 1,000 of the navy's eventual 4,660 crew members on board. We immediately recognized Elise's radiant face in the sea of uniformed sailors. After a few formalities, Ramie shared a quick embrace and a box of chocolates with her before we boarded a four-person ATV that was waiting to take us around. We drove only a few hundred feet, to the one end of the cavernous bay, before stopping.

"Welcome aboard the USS *Gerald R. Ford,*" said a man standing in front of a roped-off section of the hold. A larger-than-life statue of the carrier's namesake towered over the scene. "I am Captain McCormack, commander of this ship." His uniform looked no different from anyone else's. Mom got out of the ATV and shook his hand, having to tilt her head back to meet his gaze.

A phalanx of female sailors waited, and one by one, each thanked my mom for her military service and for paving the way for women to serve in the navy. The ship's nurses, both men and women, paid a similar tribute to Mom because she had been a nurse.

With hundreds of sailors looking on, Captain McCormack exchanged my mom's hard hat for a commanding officer's ball cap. He went on to retell everyone the story of our family's connection to Gerald R. Ford and how his assistance to Mom and Dad after the war was a representation of the former president's integrity. He pointed to the statue and asked, "What do you think, does our statue look like him?"

"No one else here is probably old enough to remember Mister Ford looking like this," Mom said as she looked over her shoulder at the image of a strapping young seaman with a full head of hair. Captain McCormack and I exchanged a smile. Indeed, I thought, most of us here remembered Ford at age sixty-two and balding, when he became the thirty-sixth president of the United States after President Richard Nixon resigned in 1974.

The formalities now concluded, we were directed back to our waiting ATV. "We would like to take you all up to the flight deck," said the captain. "There is no way to get you up there but to take one of the elevators." We looked at each other in confusion. We were picturing regular passenger elevators. It turned out the captain meant we would be going up in one of the three eighty-five-foot by fifty-two-foot elevators that were used to move aircraft from the hangar bay to the flight deck. "We have not tested this one yet," he continued, "so this will be a first for all of us." Mom just rolled her eyes and smiled. She was more than willing to be part of the exciting test run.

Many shipbuilders and sailors, all of whom were excited to see the elevator operate for the first time, accompanied us. A loud horn blasted. The platform shuddered. In a matter of seconds we were there. Our driver motored us off the elevator and onto the five-acre flight deck, driving slowly enough for the captain to comfortably walk beside us and talk. He explained that there were still a lot of things to finish before the navy could fully take command of the ship, but most of the mechanics necessary to launch fighter planes were operational. We were shown how jet exhaust was deflected by hydraulic flaps that rose from the deck at the direction of four sailors using hand signals.

"The men and women running this ship are only nineteen or twenty years old," Captain McCormack said, gesturing to the demonstration. "It gives me great pride to know that we have so many capable young people in the navy today."

I could see that it gave Mom a lot of pride too. She had been one of those twenty-year-olds who stepped up to serve their country. I also understood that it was important for Mom to see not just this next-generation aircraft carrier but also the next generation of Americans who were prepared to preserve what she had proudly fought for seventy years earlier.

Next we were shown some of the ship's cutting-edge technology, including a new catapult system. Previously powered by steam, the catapults now used electromagnetism and could propel aircraft over two hundred miles per hour over a distance of three hundred feet. We followed the catapult track's outline on the deck all the way to the bow of the ship, imagining a fighter squadron taking off for battle. "We have the capacity to fly two hundred seventy sorties a day," Captain McCormack told us. "We cannot do this on any other class of carrier."

In order to show us how the system worked, we rode to a large television monitor set up on deck for our viewing. Mom had to sit high in the seat to see the screen as a civilian engineer cued the video to show some launch tests made by President Ford's daughter, Susan, during the carrier's formal dedication. Large barge-like "sleds" replicated the weight of certain aircraft, and they were used instead of real planes to simulate the launches. "Those things make quite a splash," Mom said when she saw how far they flew off the bow after launching. We saw that they floated and bobbed in the water for later retrieval by helicopter.

Captain McCormack, a former navy pilot himself, answered all of our questions and told us about some of his firsthand experiences landing fighter jets on a moving aircraft carrier. He pointed to a pair of retractable pylons on the runway, which supported a giant net used to "catch" jets that have missed the tail hook upon landing. "That's just like being caught in a big baseball mitt," Mom said, to which he had to agree.

As our well-choreographed tour was nearing an end, we were driven over to the "island," the large superstructure that towered a hundred fifty feet over the flight deck and served as the command center for flight-deck operations as well as the ship as a whole. "Why don't we take some photos here?" the captain asked as we noticed lots of people standing around waiting.

Mom stood tall as each group lined up next to her for their photo opportunity. Afterward, we got back into the ATV and returned to the deck elevator for our ride down. We all were surprised again by how fast the one-hundred-twenty-ton elevator could move.

We exited the platform and reentered the hangar deck, where a group of shipbuilders—all military veterans—stood in a line, waiting for Mom's return from above. Each took their turn to shake her hand, proclaiming the military branch they had served in and for how long. Their combined service totaled more than two hundred years. My mom was visibly moved by the gesture, her eyes in direct contact with each man in turn as she used both of her small hands to shake their one.

Later, as we were making our way back to the minivan that had shuttled us over, members of the navy's press corps and public relations department peppered Mom with questions. Work had resumed on the hangar deck and it was so loud that I could not overhear their questions or my mom's answers.

I leaned in and could just make out one sailor asking, "What's been your favorite thing on your trip so far?"

I still tensed up a little bit whenever someone asked my mom questions. Sure, I had seen her looking great on national television and I knew she was now used to being recognized on the street, but as her son, I could not help but worry about her. Sometimes people expected a lot from her, and I knew her as a humble, quiet person. I continued to smile, but I held my breath, waiting to hear what she would utter.

Mom craned her neck so she could look straight into the eyes of the young sailor and scrunched her forehead a little as she gave the question some thought. She let out a little "Oh" and then replied, "I'd have to say this right here is. This is it!"

CHAPTER 13

Flavor

WINTHROP. MASSACHUSETTS.
TO BAR HARBOR. MAINE

MAY

[Tim]

For some reason I have always been fascinated by food—how it is cooked as well as what it looks and tastes like. I did not realize how young I was when my interest took hold until my mom, on our cross-country trip, told everyone who would listen about how I would play make-believe cooking at age two. Apparently I would tear paper into small pieces, arrange them on the hand-me-down tin plates I was given, and then present the whole thing as supper.

By the time I was nine, I was watching Julia Child on the fuzzy black-and-white screen of my parents' small television. This tall woman with the high-pitched voice and a penchant for butter captivated me. Her show, *The French Chef,* was one of the first televised cooking shows in the United States, and it introduced French cooking to the populace at a time when frozen TV dinners were all the rage. When my cousins from Cleveland, Ohio, came to visit, they could recite all the box scores from the local Indians baseball team. All I could tell them was how to make a good omelet.

My mom was not a fabulous cook. (Baker, yes. Her chocolate chip cookies and strawberry-rhubarb pies particularly stood out.) I suppose she was limited by our family budget as well as my dad's lack of interest in anything but meat and potatoes. Main-dish casseroles were very popular in the 1960s, and we had more than our fair share of them. Mom's tuna-noodle was one of the worst I can remember eating. The combination of canned tuna, cooked pasta, peas, and cream-of-mushroom soup just made me want to gag. To this day, I cannot eat tuna from a can or pouch because of the trauma. Yet cooking was a bond between us. I was always curious about what Mom was doing in the kitchen—even if I was not enamored of the product—and preparing food was something we shared as soon as I could reach the stove by standing on a stool.

A stint in my early teens of cooking for an elderly couple opened my eyes to the larger culinary world. I was doing yard work for them when the wife of the duo broke her ankle and could not cook for a while. Because of their more sophisticated palates, onions and garlic and lamb and seafood suddenly became part of my life. They would also take me out occasionally for fine dining at the social club they belonged to. While in high school, I expanded my horizons as far as they could go by frequenting some local Chinese restaurants, the most exotic cuisine that was available at the time.

My interest in food followed me through my life. Even during periods of relative poverty or a commitment to vegetarianism in my twenties, I was always able to create meals out of the food available to me, and I was always eager to share it with others. Most of us have only one or two ways to communicate and receive love. I discovered early on that food was my love language. Few things in life give me greater pleasure than to prepare a meal for someone; it is one way I can show people that I love them like family.

Now that Mom was living with me on the road, I was excited about the opportunity to explore this kind of love with her. Ramie and I also wanted her to sample all the tastes she had missed in her previous ninety years by being limited to Dad's preferences, a tight budget, and regional offerings. Before we had embarked on our adventure, we decided to try to eat a signature food from each state we visited.

In Michigan's Upper Peninsula we sampled pasties, a meat hand pie introduced to the area by Cornish miners who had migrated there in the 1800s. There was nothing inside this half-circle-shaped pastry—stuffed with diced beef, onion, potato, and rutabaga—that Mom found unappealing.

It was easy to check off the state of Wisconsin with a bag of fresh cheese curds, and with much joy we showed Mom how to make the small bites squeak in your mouth when you eat them.

None of us was up for trying lutefisk (dried codfish soaked in lye and served at room temperature), so we settled on another Minnesota classic: anything fried. We each tried a fried macaroni-and-cheese sandwich that left even my petite mom concerned for her figure.

South Dakota was trickier for us, in part because we had never heard of chislic before we looked up its state food, nor did we know where to get some. "Let's get some chislic," we would tease Mom. Hailing originally from the Caucasus, the cubed red meat—usually lamb, venison, or other wild game—is deep-fried, salted, and usually eaten with a toothpick. We settled on some award-winning microbrews instead.

After we ventured into Wyoming, it was not a hard sell to get my mom to try her first buffalo burger. "I like this better than an ordinary old hamburger," she declared as she wiped ketchup from her chin.

Our state-by-state culinary adventure hit a roadblock when we arrived in Colorado. Both Ramie and I had lived there for many years and were quite familiar with its signature dish: Rocky Mountain oysters. "Oyster" is a euphemism; they are actually deep-fried bull testicles. I knew that even if I convinced Mom to try one, I would not be able to do the same because of my aversion to any kind of offal. It seemed as though the official food-sampling adventure would have to end there, after only five states.

But then I realized that what I would miss most was not the food itself but the social and cultural elements of it. This was not just about Mom tasting new and different foods. It was about showing her the significance of what we ate, where we ate, and with whom we ate. I feel most alive when I am sharing a meal around a table with others. No other creature on Earth consumes food at a table; it is a uniquely human endeavor. Partaking of a meal with other people always reminds me that there is more to food than mere sustenance, and that feeling was what I wanted to share with my mom. From there on out, our search for regional foods took on a new dimension.

We did end up eating more classic state foods, including green chile in New Mexico, seafood gumbo in Louisiana, and grouper sandwiches in Florida. Not to mention the key lime pie research project we devised for ourselves in the Sunshine State. But by the time we started chasing spring up the Eastern Seaboard, the signature meals we tried were so much more than regional specialties; they were experiences of fellowship with people and communities who once had been strangers. And even I was unprepared for how deeply sharing a meal would connect us to the people we had just met.

◊ ◊ ◊

It was impossible to find a campground in Boston. The closest one was in Foxborough, Massachusetts, about a thirty-mile drive from Boston's historical center, and that was where we stayed for five days after we made our way up from Virginia. Ramie and I had met an old friend, Jeff, and his girlfriend, Maggie, earlier that week at the Boston Commons. We all took turns pushing my mom along the two-and-a-half-mile Freedom Trail, which winds through downtown and passes sixteen historical locations connected to the Revolutionary War and American independence. As we passed through Boston's Little Italy, we made sure to track down an authentic meatball sandwich, and Mom would not let us leave Hanover Street without a visit to Mike's Pastry for some of its famous cannoli. She did enjoy her sweets. The rest of the time we just hung out in the motor home, Mom walking behind her wheelchair around the campground loops in between reading her way through the latest stack of books we had found in the campground's clubhouse.

Two months earlier we had received a message from a sheriff's deputy outside of Boston. Sergeant Danny shared with us that he had a lot of friends who were following Miss Norma's Facebook page, and they all wanted us to stop by for a visit. A private cruise of Boston Harbor followed by a lobster and a beer were promised, an invitation Mom could hardly say no to. We kept in touch with Sergeant Danny after his initial invitation, and we telephoned him upon our arrival to say we were staying in nearby Foxborough and would be up for that visit, if his offer was still good.

"That's great, Tim," he said. "How about this weekend? We're supposed to have great weather."

"Umm, we have to be out of the campground by Friday, Danny," I truthfully replied. Indeed, the entire place was booked up in advance for the weekend.

"Well, you'll just have to come camp out in our neighborhood, then," he countered.

A little Internet research informed us that Danny's neighborhood was an oceanside Boston suburb situated at the north entrance to Boston Harbor, directly across from Logan International Airport. Located on a peninsula, Winthrop is accessed by a narrow isthmus from the west or by a bridge from East Boston. It is also one of the smallest and most densely populated municipalities in the state of Massachusetts.

"This will certainly be a challenge with the motor home," Ramie said as she zoomed in on the satellite image of the neighborhood on Google Maps. "It's really tight in there, and look at all of those trees with potentially low branches."

I had to agree as I looked over her shoulder at the computer screen. I could see only one off-street parking spot that looked even remotely large enough for our motor home with its slide-outs. Still, I was up for the adventure.

"Let's try it, Ramie," I said. "I think we can make it fit somewhere in there if we do."

After we came across the bridge into Winthrop, we could see that our worries had been unfounded. Danny had mobilized his entire neighborhood with the precision and secrecy of a SWAT operation in preparation for our arrival. His friend Louie offered us a spot to park in his driveway—a flat, open area where the motor home fit perfectly. We got our water and electricity from his neighbor Janet. "My door is open to you day and night," she told us. "You're welcome to take showers or just come in to hang out."

Fearful that word of our whereabouts would leak out and a media frenzy might occur, Danny later informed us that he had told only a few key people who was to be fêted that weekend. He had enlisted Sheryl, the wife of his good friend Scotty, to cook our first night's dinner, but had sworn Scotty to secrecy. All Sheryl knew was that someone important would be visiting and she should make one of her famous Italian feasts.

And what a feast it was. Mom sat at the head of a large table that normally seated twelve but that night held many more. There was barely enough room for a dinner plate at the table's perimeter because the center held so much food. There were platters of stuffed manicotti, giant meatballs, pasta, grilled pork loin, shrimp, and numerous vegetable dishes. The platters were quickly and frequently replenished before our eyes. A trifle that was three times the size of my mom's head appeared for dessert. Connected by this sumptuous meal was a cadre of people who had stopped by to share it. Friends, neighbors, family, a Boston assistant district attorney, and a state senator all joined with us in food and conversation that evening.

The following day, our bellies and hearts still full, we wheeled Mom through the neighborhood to Chuck and Nancy's waterfront house. Some of our new friends from the night before walked along with us, intending to join us on a tour of Boston Harbor. At the house, we were invited to head out back, where we came upon a long pier that led to Chuck's forty-six-foot yacht, *My Girls*. Our host more fully welcomed us there but then immediately apologized that he had to leave us for a catering job (he owned a large catering company in South Boston). Before he left, he introduced us to two friends he had enlisted to captain his ship: Gary, the owner of a local marine store, and Lou were master mariners. Lou, in fact, was also one of the captains of the Winthrop Ferry. We were confident that we were in good hands.

When it came time to climb aboard, I knew it would take a combined effort to get my mom up to the pilothouse. While I flanked her left side, Danny wrapped his hands around Mom's waist and steadied her up the four steps onto the boat. Scotty, who stood almost eye-to-eye with Mom as she perched on the second to last step, held tight to her other side.

It was a beautiful sunny day. We spent time on the deck talking to new friends and taking in the Boston Harbor sights. When we returned to shore three hours later, we paused in the water at the end of an airport runway as jet planes descended, buzzing only a few feet over the yacht's deck as they noisily landed at Logan International. We all waved to the passengers, who could be seen clearly through the airliner's windows.

Sun-kissed and glowing from the events of the past twenty-four hours, we returned to the motor home for a short rest, and then it was time for our promised lobster. We followed Danny to Belle Isle Seafood, a local favorite for many years. As I wheeled Mom in the door, we were immediately greeted by a packed house of well-wishers, including children holding handmade signs saying WELCOME TO BOSTON, MISS NORMA.

Jimmy, the owner, steamed his largest lobster for Mom, and then he and Danny stood next to her, tying a plastic bib with a bright red lobster design around her neck while her face beamed. These two grown men sat on either side of my diminutive mom and helped her make her way through the biggest lobster I had ever seen by cracking the shell, extracting the meat, and handing her the pieces for easy eating. While she was up to her elbows in drawn butter, she looked at me with a greasy smile and simply said, "Good!"

After she had finished the lobster, I could see that she was full and at ease, talking to some young girls, so I let myself fall into a conversation with Jimmy. For almost a full hour we talked about our mothers, life, death, and everything in between—really personal stuff for a couple of guys who had just met each other.

"I've never had that long of a conversation with Jimmy in the ten years I've known him," Danny later told me. When I looked for Jimmy as we were leaving, I learned that he had retreated to the kitchen with tears in his eyes. I asked his wife, Stephanie, if he could come out to say good-bye, but she quietly shook her head no. "He is too emotional to face you as you leave," she told us. "He doesn't want to say good-bye."

The next day was Sunday, and that meant it was time for us to continue our way northward. We wanted to avoid the busy Boston traffic we knew would commence again the following workday. As we secured everything in the motor home, I thought about all the people we had met during our short stay. But most of all, I thought about the food, the Italian feast, the lobster. Besides providing us with electricity and water, Janet had also set out a breakfast buffet both mornings as well as lunch. And I reflected on how effortlessly I had shared my deepest feelings with people I had met only a few hours earlier, and how sincerely that openness had been returned.

The day we were leaving, Janet excused herself to "run some

errands," but unbeknownst to us, she went instead to the Winthrop police station to arrange a police escort out of town. Two cruisers arrived shortly afterward and did just that.

Ready to go, we all said teary good-byes. Ringo dug his paws into the ground, unwilling to leave his new friend Lou and join us in the motor home. With flashing lights and siren chirps at the intersections, we were led through Winthrop's narrow streets and to the edge of town. When we stopped the motor home at the city limits, one officer came to say that we were at the end of their jurisdiction and they would have to leave us. I leaned out the driver's side window to shake his hand. "Thank you for doing what you are doing," he said as tears streamed down his face, reluctant to let my hand go.

◊ ◊ ◊

From Winthrop, we traveled toward Acadia National Park in Maine, which was the northernmost point of our trip up the Atlantic Seaboard. We continued to catch glimpses of spring as tree buds began to leaf out and some early blooming flowers discreetly showed themselves. Our timing was perfect; the vacationer crowds would not arrive for a few more weeks. We took day trips to the park from our waterfront campground on the western end of Mount Desert Island, enjoying the solitude the place afforded after such a busy weekend with Sergeant Danny and the rest of the Winthrop community.

One morning toward the end of our stay on the island, a message in the *Driving Miss Norma* in-box, from someone named Lisa, had caught my eye: "Last year my father was diagnosed with cancer. I read *Being Mortal,* and I found your journey. I am convinced that I discovered all in that order for a reason. I work for Friends of Acadia (our office is in downtown Bar Harbor) and I have been following you joyfully for some time now. I would love to meet you before you leave. There is a great pancake place on Cottage Street in Bar Harbor. I can be there by 8 a.m. Do you have time?"

I glanced at my watch; it was too late to meet Lisa for pancakes. We had already planned on another visit to Acadia National Park that day, though, and our route there would take us right through the charming town of Bar Harbor.

"This woman sounds cool," I told Ramie. "She works for Friends of Acadia, a nonprofit conservation organization. We should try to somehow hook up with her today."

"Why don't we just drop in on her at work after our park visit?" Ramie answered. "We can surprise her!"

Emboldened by our collective experiences with strangers, we were by now quite practiced in following our instincts when it came to meeting new people. Sometimes we even went out of our way to meet them. Today would be one of those days.

Not too long after reading Lisa's message, I parked the Jeep a block down from her organization's headquarters. Mom and I waited as Ramie ran in to see if Lisa was there. Ramie returned very shortly to tell us that she was not. "Her coworkers say that she is doing tai chi at the local YMCA," Ramie informed us. "Let's go looking for her."

Mom and I stood outside the single-story recreational facility on the other side of town as Ramie went in to inquire about tai chi classes. Lisa's class happened to be practicing in front of a window that faced our way, and while she was in the middle of a posture, she saw us standing outside. A huge smile of recognition graced her face, and she ran out of the building and rushed toward Mom.

"How did you find me?" she exclaimed.

We filled her in on our detective work and chatted a bit until Lisa realized that she had to get ready to go back to work. Not wanting to finish our talk, she added, "Why don't you guys join me and my family for dinner tonight? Do you like seafood stew?"

We did not say a word to each other; we did not have to. I gave Mom and Ramie a quick glance and then said, "We love seafood stew. What time would you like us to come?"

Lisa, her husband, Bob, and their young daughter, Grace, lived on a part of the island where the tourists do not go. We nearly got lost as we drove deep into the thick forest before coming into a small clearing that was only slightly larger than their three-story hand-built house. We marveled at the smooth dome roof and were enchanted before we even entered the charming abode.

Once inside, we were greeted with the yeasty aroma of fresh-baked bread. The stew vegetables were already peeled and slowly coming to a boil on the stove, and a platter of fresh seafood awaited entry into the pot. At the eat-in kitchen table, Ramie and Mom shared with Bob stories of our adventures, while in another room, Grace played with Ringo.

I did what I always do: headed for the stove. As I tried to make myself helpful, Lisa opened up to me about her dad's fight with mesothelioma and how it was affecting her. Standing there in the middle of her kitchen, with the sound of knives slicing through salad fixings on wooden cutting boards, the stew simmering, and relaxed voices floating through the house, Lisa and I shared many stories. Soon we shared tears and hugs too as we both connected to our feelings about our parents' health crises. Lisa told me she wished her father was up for a trip like my mom's, but sadly, he was not. She tried to visit him as often as possible, however, to create some positive end-of-life memories of her own.

We lingered at Lisa's house long after dinner, not wanting the laughter and the love to come to an end. Six-year-old Grace was clearly ready for more action since she disappeared upstairs. Upon her return she was carrying her soaking-wet cat. "Here, Miss Norma, I just gave my kitty a bath. You can hold her now!" she said as she tried to set the kitten on Mom's lap. The room exploded with laughter. It felt so good to share such ordinary moments with people we barely knew.

Eventually Mom starting yawning and I knew it was time to leave. When we said our good-byes, Lisa and I promised each other we would stay in touch.

A peaceful silence fell over us as we made our way out of the forest and onto an asphalt road that eventually led us back to the campground. Ramie was curled up in the passenger seat, and in the rearview mirror I could see Mom and Ringo snuggled in the back. I felt so full—full of good food in my body and such love in my heart.

As I drove, my mind wandered back over the many meals we had had across the South and up the East Coast. I laughed to my-self, remembering Mom trying raw oysters in New Orleans in November. At first she had given us her typical response when we proposed the idea at Felix's Restaurant and Oyster Bar: "Oh, I don't know about that." But we had ordered them every which way anyway: some raw, others grilled, still others Rockefeller style.

When they were brought to the table, Mom reluctantly agreed to try one of each. She happily ate the cooked ones, but when it was time for the raw one, we could see her slightly hesitate.

"I don't know about this," she said again as she peered at the grey mass that occupied the half shell. Then, with a glint in her eye, she decided to just go for it as our waitress busied herself nearby. Mom tilted back her head and slid the oyster into her mouth, its slimy texture eliciting a slight grimace. Undeterred, she slurped it down and said, "That's not so bad."

The waitress waltzed over and in her thick Southern drawl said, "Honey, you are a lot braver than I am. I have worked here for eighteen years and I have never tried one of those."

Mom just beamed and then slurped down another.

Still driving toward our campground, the roads mostly empty and the sky turning darker and darker, I also thought about the meal we had had at the North Beach Grill on Tybee Island, a recommendation from a Facebook follower who had encouraged us to stop by and visit "Big George." I could see the colorful beach-shack restaurant in my mind's eye. I could also remember the sound of the wind blowing through the palm trees by the outdoor deck that overlooked the white-sand beach where the Savannah River meets the Atlantic Ocean.

While we had waited for our drinks, we noticed a bald African American man, wearing a ball cap and a wide smile, get up from where he sat at a table near the kitchen door. *This must be Big George,* I thought. At least six feet six inches tall and of equally large proportions, he wore blue jeans and a red, white, and blue polo shirt with a Ralph Lauren logo. The big man sauntered across the bare-wood floor and took a place at our table next to my mom. Her whole body fit into the curve of his large arm as he placed it around her.

"Well, you must be Miss Norma," he said in a soft Southern voice that belied his size. "I just read all about you."

Mom blushed and nodded her head. "Why, yes, I am," she replied.

"The guys and I were just looking at your Facebook page," he said. "You sure do get around."

Soon Big George was explaining to us why there were so many "guys" and no women waiting tables at his popular bar and restaurant: he preferred to hire down-on-their-luck young men. Big George not only gave these guys employment but mentored them and gave them love and respect; he was sort of like a foster parent to them. Mom could identify with that. I could tell she took an instant liking to him by the way she leaned back comfortably into his arm.

Over the course of our meal, Big George came by our table again to sit with us, talking and joking with Mom, asking us if we liked our food and eventually suggesting some house-made chocolate-caramel cake for dessert. By the end of the evening, we had all been laughing together as if we were old friends. He had insisted on picking up our tab and had invited us to come by and see him again before we left Tybee Island.

Now nearly back to the motor home, I began to remember the faces of everyone I had cried with while we had been on the East Coast—people I had only just met. But with food spread out before us to share, we had all felt safe enough to dive right in to the big stuff: loss, family, the meaning of life. Discussions on how to give our parents a good end-of-life, how it feels to take care of loved ones who are ill or aging, how scary it is to talk about death and to be faced with our vulnerability as human beings. It had not mattered if we were visiting a whole community or just one family; I had found such authentic and supportive connections with people over tables and kitchen islands bursting with food.

I checked the rearview mirror again and saw that Mom was fast asleep and that Ringo had his head on her lap and was sleeping too. It had been many years since I made those make-believe suppers out of paper for her and since I needed a step stool to work next to her at the stove. My whole life I had wanted to express my love to others through the medium of food. I had just no idea how much love would come back to me—and to my mom—in the kitchen.

CHAPTER 14

Balance

PITTSBURGH. PENNSYLVANIA. TO
YELLOWSTONE NATIONAL PARK. WYOMING

JUNE AND JULY

[Ramie]

We spent the spring eating our way across the northeastern part of the country and then headed toward western Pennsylvania, landing at my childhood home and old stomping grounds just in time for the onset of summer. This stop had been long scheduled—we had aimed the motor home in this direction in order to participate in the happiest of occasions: my best friend from childhood was getting married.

This was the friend who had gathered us teenage girls on New Year's Eve in 1982 to have a break-dancing party in her parents' kitchen; the one who had nervously come out to me over twenty years ago, telling me what I had already known for a long time; the one who had made sure spectacular gifts were delivered to an out-of-the-way campground in the California desert on my fiftieth birthday; and the one who had been on the other end of the phone as we navigated through the extraordinary journey we called "Driving Miss Norma."

I was thrilled to have the honor of being asked to officiate Patti and April's wedding. And so, as June eighteenth drew near, we settled into Bear Run Campground and spent a few weeks preparing for the event. Tim's gift to the brides was to cater the affair. Mine was to do whatever I could to support them through this exciting time, remove any stress, and eventually facilitate a beautiful ceremony.

Up until June, we had enjoyed a storybook journey. Norma had been up for nearly everything that came our way, and her health had seemed to improve rather than decline. Her medications were under control, and her energy level remained high. She had steadily been gaining some weight from all the delicious food we had explored together, and her cheeks were rosy from time spent out in the sun. She continued to be a joy to be around. We had our share of ups and downs, to be sure, but the shock we had experienced back in Presque Isle almost a year before seemed miles and miles away from us now. Things had seemed to go our way more often than not. We were on top of it, we thought.

A week before the wedding, Norma, Tim, and I returned to the motor home after a fun day with Patti, enjoying more great food in the Strip District and riding the incline on Mount Washington overlooking downtown Pittsburgh. We opened the door to find our sweet poodle was not quite himself. We thought maybe Ringo had something stuck in his throat, but the more we watched, the more it became clear that something was seriously wrong. He ignored his favorite treats and tried to regurgitate with no success. His head was heavy and his eyes were unfocused.

We quickly Googled "emergency vet near me" and then Tim and I took off in the Jeep for the longest twenty-minute drive of our lives. Norma stayed behind in the motor home. We were in such a hurry we did not even pause long enough to let her know what was going on. It troubled us to leave her alone, but our worry was now totally focused on Ringo.

X-rays revealed that Ringo's stomach had twisted and he had bloat. "He is about to die," the straightforward Dr. Wilson told us. "His only hope is immediate surgery." She spoke with a not-so-hopeful tone, as if she had been burned by optimism in the past.

The veterinary staff asked Tim and me many of the same questions we had discussed with Norma over the past few months. "If he goes into cardiac arrest, do you want us to give him CPR?" "How much are you willing to spend for treatment?" "Do you want him cremated if we can't save him?" It was an excruciating process. These were the same big life-and-death questions we had for so long skirted around with Norma, and although it had taken some time to tackle them head-on, we at least had some time to think about them first. Here, again, the same questions were thrown at us, rapidly and unexpectedly, about our Ringo boy.

However, I was surprised to realize that all our answers on behalf of Ringo were not exactly the same as Norma's. Ringo was part of our family—he was our stabilizer, our therapy poodle when no one else could possibly understand. He could not die. Not now.

"Oh God" was all I could utter through my tight chest.

A young veterinary technician came in with a two-page cost itemization for his potentially life-saving surgery. She started reading from the top, a long list of things that I could barely hear or process. Tim must have felt the same way. He interrupted her, saying, "Just show me the bottom line—time is of the essence." It was a lot of money. There were no guarantees. We signed anyway, unable to imagine life without Ringo.

In Tim's pocket was an uncashed check. He had inherited a car from his sister eight years before, and in the spirit of downsizing, we had recently sold it. It was for the exact amount of the estimate. We felt certain that once again Stacy had found a way to make sure we were taken care of.

Ringo was prepped for surgery, and with an IV in his left front leg, he wagged his tail as we said good night and maybe good-bye.

Back in the car, I looked over at Tim as he put the key into the ignition. His eyes were puffy and red. *Mine must be too,* I thought. My stomach churned and my hands were shaking. I thought I might be sick. Tim was barely able to drive back to the campground through his tears. We were a mess.

We poured ourselves up the motor home's steps and gave over to uncontrollable sobbing when we hit the couch next to where Norma sat. We had never left her alone like that without an explanation, but upon our return we found she was completely unfazed, acting like we had never been gone. In fact, she was much more at ease than we were. Tim slowly shared the dire situation, in bits and pieces, his voice breaking as he went back over the details. "It doesn't look good, Mom," he finished. "But we have no idea what will happen," and he began to sob again. He reached his hand out for mine and we both sat there, inconsolable and wrecked.

"*Listen,*" Norma said.

The sound of her voice shocked me out of my crying and I looked up at her, curious. Her voice had been loud and firm, but she had not yelled. I glanced at Tim, who seemed even more surprised than I was, and then back at the suddenly commanding woman across from me.

"You have to be positive," she demanded. "Ringo needs you to be positive and know he will be all right. You're doing him no good otherwise."

It was way past nine o'clock when we quietly walked Norma to bed without our usual singing and dancing. Inspired by the strength of her conviction, we tried to pull ourselves together. There was no way we were going to fall asleep until we heard from the veterinary hospital. Three hours of restlessness ended when my ringtone sounded.

"I have Ringo opened up, and there is good news," Dr. Wilson explained. "There is no damage to his spleen. You got him here just in time."

Tim and I strained to hear what Dr. Wilson was telling us over the breaking-up connection, our cheeks tightly pressed together against the shared cell phone. Our tears mingled as they streamed down, dampening the carpet below.

"So is he going to be okay?" I asked hopefully.

"He isn't out of the woods yet," she cautioned. "His stomach and all his organs look good, but we never know how these big dogs will react coming out of the anesthesia. For now, no news is good news. You guys get some sleep. I won't call until morning unless there is a complication. I just wanted you to know how he is doing so far." The surgeon sounded tired and confident while still avoiding any sense of false hope.

We must have been holding our breaths because the moment the call ended we both deeply exhaled.

With no sleep and plenty of affirmative prayers, time passed. The morning call was good news. Ringo had survived the surgery and was recovering nicely. "We still need to keep an eye on him for a couple of days, but you can come and visit if you would like," the receptionist told us.

"We'll be there in thirty minutes," Tim replied.

Relief washed over us when Ringo hobbled into the visiting room, doped up and confused. We delicately ran our fingers through his soft, fuzzy coat and held him close. Ringo's close call with death was a wake-up call. It was then that we realized we were not immune to bad things happening to us after all.

◊ ◊ ◊

The following week was hard for all of us. Ringo turned his nose up at his special dog food prescribed by the veterinarian, so Tim began to make homemade doggie stew in addition to all our food. We juggled Ringo's four-times-a-day medicine routine with Norma's needs and then our own.

The day of the wedding, I arose early to photograph the brides in the golden morning light. It was a perfect early summer day: sunny and warm but not hot, not a cloud in the sky, not even a hint of rain—exactly how every bride dreams her wedding day will be. It was just we three girls, laughing, having a great time, and creating the keepsakes that would hopefully last them a lifetime.

After the photo shoot, I returned to the campground in time to help Norma with her morning routine, quickly crossing paths with Tim as he hurried out to get the buffet ready for a hundred twenty excited guests. We had timed it so both Norma and Ringo would be cared for seamlessly.

Norma had picked out her wedding outfit long beforehand, and she took a little extra time before coming out of her bedroom, dressed and ready to go, even with a dab of pink lipstick for the special occasion. Something seemed different, though. Her affect was flat. Her trademark smile had been erased from her face. Something more like a grimace had replaced it.

"How are you on this beautiful morning?" I asked, trying to disguise the worry in my voice.

Her gaze met the floor and she said, "Not so good today."

This was something new. In the ten months we had been on the road with her, I had not seen her this dispirited.

She was short of breath, she said. She also had an unfamiliar pain in her stomach. She looked scared. Was it the cancer pressing on something, causing discomfort? Was her heart giving out? Had some disease moved into her lungs? It was hard to tell, but the shift was palpable. She was not comfortable, she was frightened, and, as always, she did not want to be a burden.

I still could not help but selfishly think, *You have got to be kidding me! This is the one day we have been focused on for months. This is a day for me to be present for my friends. We made it through the Ringo crisis and now this?* I was tired. We all were.

Then I wondered whether she secretly had an issue with gay marriage that she had not revealed until now. Maybe she was so shy that a physical manifestation of an illness was the only thing she thought would get her out of this uncomfortable social situation. Or was she really sick? Maybe dying? What should I do?

We needed to talk it through.

"Let's sit down together for a minute, Norma," I told her. "Are you uncomfortable with the wedding of two women?" I asked.

"Oh no. I'm very excited for the girls," she replied. "I'm just not feeling well today."

I told her I was not comfortable leaving her in the motor home by herself all day and into the night. She agreed to come to the house and stay inside since the wedding festivities were going to be outdoors. We both knew it was not ideal, but short of canceling the wedding, it was our only option. We were just six short hours away from "I do."

I helped Ringo down a borrowed ramp out of the motor home and into my mom's minivan, careful not to tear his delicate stitches. Norma was next. I held her hand down the five steps, helped her into her chair, wheeled her to the car, boosted her into the front seat, then packed both the ramp and wheelchair into the back of the van. Ten miles away, I reversed the procedure and settled in both my patients just as the wedding guests were arriving for appetizers and drinks.

The ceremony was performed under a beautifully symmetrical old oak tree in the far corner of Patti and April's rural property. Stained-glass panels hung from the tree's substantial branches and turned Mother Nature into a stunning cathedral. The guests filtered in, each finding their place on quilt-covered hay bales. The love and celebration were overwhelming as my friends walked through the field and joined me at the tree. Somehow this moment seemed intensely significant—none of us had ever participated in a gay wedding until now.

Later we heard over and over again how lovely the wedding had been. Some said that they had never experienced such an honest, personal, and real ceremony that reflected the couple's personalities so accurately. "Love was celebrated today!" one guest said. "Ramie, you nailed it," said another. Nobody knew that I was an absolute mess, frustrated that Norma did not have the energy to witness this beautiful event and worried that something was truly wrong with her. I wanted to will her to sit up under the magnificent oak tree and celebrate love. After all, love was really what our trip together so far was all about.

Instead, as we found out later, her heart was failing.

◊ ◊ ◊

"I don't want to see any doctors," Norma said again the day after the wedding. We were sitting outside the motor home, a warm summer breeze cooling the air, trying to convince her that she needed to go to a hospital. We usually respected her wishes, but her health seemed so fragile that we could stand it no longer. There was a fine line in our minds between rejecting the medical community and needlessly suffering. Both her legs were swollen from the knees down and she was having trouble breathing. Tim and I could see that she was slowly drowning in her own fluids.

"Maybe there's something that can make you feel better," I pleaded with her. "Let's just at least have the problem diagnosed. We won't let the doctors do anything you don't want them to do," we promised. Three days after the wedding, she reluctantly agreed.

As we wheeled Norma through the hospital doors, memories of Leo's last days were front and center.

"When was the last time you saw a doctor?" the intake nurse asked Norma. Tim and I looked at each other when Norma truthfully answered. "You haven't seen a doctor in ten months?" the nurse chided while moving her gaze to us. Her tone had a bite that made us all feel uncomfortable. Up until then, we had always felt right supporting Norma's choices for her end-of-life care.

Just the day before, our story had been featured on the front page of Pittsburgh's largest newspaper, the *Post-Gazette*. "Miss Norma makes a 'Pitt'stop in Pittsburgh," the headline read. Clearly the hospital staff had not read yesterday's paper.

Blood samples were taken and tests were run. Preliminary results indicated that Norma was suffering from congestive heart failure and arterial fibrillation. The attending physician suggested that we keep her overnight for observation. Tim and Norma both made it clear they did not want that.

Tim implored, "I watched both my sister and my father spend their last days in a hospital. This isn't how my mom is going out."

Norma looked up at the harried doctor from her frail, failing body and stated, "I'm not staying here."

"Perhaps now would be a good time to have a conversation with Norma about dying and her end-of-life wishes," the doctor advised us. Tim and I suddenly felt vindicated after our shame only a few moments before. We were one step ahead of them on that one.

We explained why we were far from her doctors and about the choices Norma had made when she had received her cancer diagnosis. We asked the hospital physician for interventions that might alleviate some of the symptoms and make it easier for her to breathe. We made it clear that heart surgery and heroics were not on the table.

There seemed to be an immediate shift in the medical staff's attitude. The nurse took me and Tim out into the hall, apologized for questioning our lack of medical care, and celebrated our support of Norma. She exuded both vulnerability and frustration. "I wish I could have more conversations with families like I am having with you," she said as she alluded to the difficulty many families have with end-of-life decisions.

About an hour later we wheeled Norma back out to the car, armed with a prescription for a week's worth of diuretics that would help reduce the fluid buildup. The confidence boost the newly supportive hospital staff had given us did not seem to last very long once we got outside. Norma's heart was failing. There was no getting around it. She was dying. I felt determined as never before to live for the moment—this very moment.

◊ ◊ ◊

From Pennsylvania we continued to make our way west across the northern part of the country, stopping in parking lots, at friends' homes, and sometimes at RV parks as we went. We spent a couple of weeks at Norma's Michigan home before we headed for the San Juan Islands in Washington State, where some beach buddies from the Baja had invited us to stay with them for a while.

On a Saturday morning in July, NBC's *Today* show found a four-and-a-half-minute slot, in between the Republican and Democratic conventions, to air Miss Norma's story. A producer/videographer had shot some background footage while we were in North Carolina, and she returned with Craig Melvin to film the interview segment only recently at a friend's bar in Dearborn, Michigan. We had spent the night in a Walmart parking lot in Minnesota's Amish country. It was well before nine o'clock in the morning and Norma was still sleeping in her room. Tim and I excitedly sat watching the show via satellite TV as the sound of horse-drawn buggies clip-clopped their way past us on the road outside. We were smiling and tearing up as Norma's interview with Craig began.

About a minute into our big network TV moment, *bam!* A crash had come from Norma's room.

I yelled, "She fell!" but Tim was already thrusting open Norma's sliding door. She was flat on her back on the floor. She was scared.

"Did she hit her head?" I yelled to Tim as I fought to get myself out of the partially deflated mattress and race toward them.

"Can you move, Mama?" Tim asked her. "Is anything broken? Are you bleeding?"

"I'm just so dizzy," she whimpered.

"Mom, what happened?"

"I was making my bed and plop. I just fell backward. I couldn't stop myself," Norma said, surprised that her body had failed her.

Tim held her head as I held her hand. At the same time we all noticed that her leg was bleeding pretty badly. Her old skin was paper thin, and she had landed on the metal latch that kept the bathroom door from moving while we were driving. Otherwise, likely thanks to decades of taking bone-enhancing vitamins and the relatively soft floor, there were no broken bones.

Tim was able to help her up. She was shaken to her core. I assessed the deep cut on her leg, cleaned and dressed it, and we fussed around her a little while longer until she seemed calm. Tim encouraged his mom to take her time getting dressed.

By the time Norma was ready for the day, doubled up on her CBD supplement, pain-free, and with very little appetite, the West Coast airing of NBC's *Today* show came on the television. Norma was illuminated from the inside out the moment she saw a larger-than-life image of herself on the set of the show in New York City. The trauma from the fall she had had just an hour earlier seemed to have evaporated.

Later, the three of us soaked in the hundreds of messages that poured in on our Facebook page following the airing. They lifted our spirits at the perfect time. We were in need of a little extra love as we made our way along I-94 to North Dakota that day.

"I am so thankful for you," Tim said to me as we settled into Bismarck for the night and after Norma had gone to sleep. "I can drive, prepare all our meals, wash the dishes, and dump the wastewater, but I don't know if I can be the person who deals with my mother's wounds. I think that bloody leg would have done me in."

In his voice I could hear how much we both knew we were entering a different phase of caregiving. I could handle the bloody leg, but could I handle the rest? I stayed up a little later than usual just staring at the ceiling and thinking about what had been and what must be coming. Balloon rides and mountain climbing might be behind us now, I realized. New challenges awaited.

◊ ◊ ◊

In late July we were in southwestern Montana when we decided to take a spontaneous side trip to Mammoth Hot Springs in Yellowstone National Park. Tim and I had been there before and thought it might be the right time to get off the interstate and enjoy one of our favorite national parks again.

We left the motor home in Livingston, Montana, for the day and loaded into the Jeep. Norma was as excited as she got in those days. She continued to be wobbly and unsure of herself. She had started to use more sign language and fewer words.

The closer we got to Mammoth and the trails we needed to hike to see the springs, I could not help but flash back to only a few short months ago when we were in Florida. Norma had been able to walk the old stone steps of the Saint Augustine fort so she could see the view over the cannons out to the Matanzas River and beyond. She had been so excited to catch this and so many other sights that nothing could have stopped her. Sure, she had been a bit more tired the next day, but she would have done it again in a heartbeat.

Things had changed after the fall. Norma had grown more tentative with each step. She seemed more dependent on her familiar handholds throughout the motor home in hopes of keeping steady. Her confidence had been diminished. She still had plenty of enthusiasm to see remarkable things, but there was no way she would march up more than the five steps required to get into the motor home. Afraid she might fall again, Norma increasingly insisted that she ride in her wheelchair instead of even trying to walk.

Tim and I both knew that a fall was usually the beginning of the end—a broken hip, a bumped head, or, in Leo's case, a compression fracture in his back. We had been lucky, because other than a flesh wound, Norma had not severely hurt herself, but it definitely signaled a change. We had been full-time care-givers before, but now the intensity of the care was ratcheting its way up.

I often found myself telling Tim, "Remember, we signed up for this. We knew this day would come." I was saying it out loud as much to convince myself as for his benefit. Knowing this day had been coming and having it here were two very different things. I really did not know if I was ready for this. I did not know if I would ever be ready.

I sighed and leaned my head against the passenger side window as the Jeep motored south down Wyoming Highway 89. As much as the beauty of the mountains and clear rocky streams tried to temper my angst, fear and worry took over my thoughts.

What will happen? How will we manage? Can we do this—in a motor home? I longed to steel myself against the reality that these changes meant, or to send the worry off on the wings of the birds flying high above me.

By the time we arrived in Mammoth, the area was packed with vehicles. We made several loops around the six or seven crowded parking lots, but everything was full. Finally we were able to pull into an accessible spot near the restrooms.

Norma, who had been quiet for most of the ride, flashed her trademark grin, and as Tim hung the blue-and-white handicap placard on the rearview mirror, she teased with her now familiar saying, "I bet you are glad you brought me along now, aren't you?"

We found that there were only a couple of wheelchair-accessible boardwalks available to view the intricate travertine terraces from, and Tim and I were slightly disappointed. We could see that most of the springs were well above us.

A fellow visitor must have recognized our adventurous spirit and pointed us to a paved path that led to the upper tier. "There are no steps, but it is really steep. If you are up for pushing up the hill, the views are worth it," she said.

As we approached the bottom of the incline, we encountered plenty of naysayers. "It's pretty steep. I wouldn't risk it," warned one passerby. And from another, "You must have more legs than brains!"

When asked if she wanted to push on, Norma just said, "Sure, let's go for it. Why not?"

"I'd be even more worried about coming back down," we heard as we began our ascent. The comments continued, but we kept going. I looked at Tim as he leaned into his mom's wheelchair and put one foot in front of the other. A smile filled his entire face.

When we arrived at the top of the hill, I took a deep breath and put my hands on the handle of Norma's wheelchair. When I looked out across historic Fort Yellowstone with its mountainous backdrop, our silver Jeep with the bright yellow and orange kayaks on top caught my eye. I remembered the sparkle in Norma's gaze as she had teased us about the parking spot. Even with all the scary events of the past two months, I thought, even with all my fears about what would happen next, Norma was right. We were so glad to have her along.

CHAPTER 15

Change

FRIDAY HARBOR, WASHINGTON

AUGUST AND SEPTEMBER

[Ramie]

The motor home calmly chugged through the seemingly end-less apple orchards of eastern Washington and up through the high peaks of North Cascades National Park, a rare spot on the map that neither Tim nor I had previously visited. We wanted to take our time and be swept away by the striking beauty we saw around us.

As we passed Diablo Lake, the surrounding tall craggy peaks were reflected in a tea of glacial till so brilliantly turquoise that it did not look real. Ordinarily, we would have pulled over, found a hiking trail, and commenced our exploration of the area. In-stead, Norma was propped up on the reclining sofa behind the driver's seat, feeling nauseated and short of breath. Reaching sea level was now our immediate goal. We thought if we returned to a lower elevation she might be more comfortable with the increased oxygen. Our only option was to get over these mountains as expeditiously as possible.

We decided to spend a couple of nights at a waterfront RV park on Fidalgo Island so that Norma could acclimate before we drove the motor home and the Jeep onto the ferry and to our intended destination: the San Juan Archipelago. It was here that we planned to spend a week or two with Nan and Steve, two Baja California friends who lived just outside Friday Harbor, Washington.

Norma's ailments seemed to clear up quickly once we were settled in at nearly sea level. Soon she was walking behind her wheelchair around the six acres we were temporarily calling home. Her leg wound from the fall the week before was healing nicely, and Tim and I both felt that her health was improving. Things might be looking up, I thought.

Nan had our visit all planned out. Our first stop would be to meet Popeye, the local harbor seal that hung out at the Friday Harbor docks near the seafood store. We would go to a farmers' market on Saturday morning and then listen to big-band music downtown on Sunday evening. There were weekly ukulele gatherings on Tuesdays with beer and popcorn, and Norma had to be included in that too. We also thought we would accept a few Facebook invitations, like whale watching, a lavender farm visit, and a play date for Ringo with another Standard Poodle named Ringo, before we moved on.

In between these outings, Norma would read, play games on her iPad, and continue to work on her suntan. It was August, the best time to visit the Pacific Northwest, an ordinarily cloudy and wet place. In the midst of a record-breaking heat wave across the entire United States, we were in the most comfortable spot—seventy-five degrees and sunny was working well for us.

Life was good. Until it was not good. Norma fell again in the night while trying to return to bed from the bathroom, which was only a couple of steps away. She was not injured, but Tim and I realized that our grand adventure might soon be coming to an end. She was sleeping more and more during the day, and we were all up more and more during the night for her frequent need to urinate. We were begging her to drink enough water for fear of dehydration but were horrified to see her legs swelling up. It was a balance that just could not be met. We thought that by now she was truly suffering from congestive heart failure and was effectively drowning in her own fluids.

Norma's decline was steady and marked. There was no sign of cancer from either her perspective or ours. She had stopped bleeding months ago, and any pain she experienced was completely controlled by her CBD pills. It was becoming clear that she would probably die of heart failure before she died of cancer.

On August 24th, we celebrated our first anniversary on the road together. There were plenty of milestones that year: thirteen thousand miles driven, thirty-two states traveled, fifteen national parks visited, plenty of new experiences, new friends made, and a whole lot of beer and cake consumed. We had a little party on Nan and Steve's trellis-covered patio, and they played their ukuleles and serenaded us with a beautiful rendition of "All the Good People" before we enjoyed two kinds of cake and a beer, as was now our tradition.

We reminisced about our year together in the motor home and shared stories from across the country with Nan and Steve. We laughed about the many times she had asked "I bet you are glad you brought me along now, aren't you?" and we basked in the friendship and hospitality of our hosts. But even in the midst of this impromptu celebration, I could somehow feel our joy beginning to mingle with heartache. We all began to understand that we were settled on San Juan Island for a completely different reason than we had first thought; this was where Norma would eventually die.

◊ ◊ ◊

As days were crossed off Norma's pocket calendar, her excessive sleepiness continued. She also was suddenly no longer interested in jigsaw puzzles, reading, or playing games on her iPad, pastimes she had truly enjoyed. She was continually short of breath, and her legs were collecting more and more fluid.

It was now becoming quite a chore to get her into and out of the motor home. We borrowed a portable oxygen generator from Nan's visiting daughter, who had occasional breathing problems, to see if she might feel better with more oxygen. At first, Norma did not want anything to do with the machine and resisted our efforts to get her to use it. I believe she interpreted it as a life-support device, not a comfort-keeping tool. After three days of refusal, she allowed us to place the cannula into her nose for a short trial. It did not take long to notice that she was breathing more easily, and she liked the feeling of oxygen reaching her vital organs enough to be more willing to use it.

When Nan's daughter planned to leave in a few days with her portable oxygen generator in tow, Norma decided that perhaps comfortable breathing was a good thing to continue. It was time to ask for help. We remembered our conversation with the Michigan doctor who had diagnosed Norma over a year ago. At the time, Tim had asked him, "What can we expect as her disease progresses and what is the best way to care for her?"

He had told us our best bet would be to seek support from a local hospice organization anywhere we found ourselves in the country. "She should be able to live out her life in your motor home."

We made an appointment at Peace Island Medical Center, the local hospital, to see if it really was that easy to get hospice support. As fate would have it, the nurse practitioner who examined Norma that morning was a former hospice nurse, and she completely understood our situation.

After an hour-long talk, we all returned to the lobby feeling quite satisfied; we had received a referral to Hospice Care of the Northwest. Tim and I could now have the support we needed to hold up our end of the bargain: Norma finishing her life in her "home."

Tim pushed his mom through the lobby, which resembled an art museum more than a hospital, and out through the automatic double doors. The three of us collectively stole some extra oxygen from the fresh Washington air. I felt such a sense of peace as I reminded myself that the endeavor we had undertaken was a marathon, not a sprint. "We can do this," I said to Tim under my breath.

We were barely outside when I looked up and suddenly gasped. There in the hospital's *porte cochere* was an idling 1980s-vintage grey Toyota MR2 with a driver obviously waiting to pick someone up. Without saying a word or even looking at each other, Tim and I slightly paused in our steps, overcome with emotion; the coincidence made it appear to us as though Leo was ready for Norma to join him in the afterlife and he was going to drive her to the other side in Mister 2. Tim picked up his pace and wheeled his mom past the car and straight to our nearby Jeep, as if to say, "Not yet, Dad."

Then we drove directly into Friday Harbor to visit the San Juan County Fair. No one would have ever guessed that Norma had just been referred to hospice care. She thoroughly inspected the blue-ribbon vegetables and pies. She cheerfully smiled and waved back at some people who recognized her when she poked her head through the holes of a plywood depiction of artist Grant Wood's *American Gothic* for a photograph. Most importantly, she was able to indulge and have an "elephant ear"—a large piece of fried dough covered with powdered sugar—which she remembered eating in her youth.

My mind was spinning like the Ferris wheel at the heart of the fair. I felt the joy of the present moment that Norma was clearly living in as well as the angst of not having the slightest idea what the next few weeks and months would look like for us.

"Welcome to Miss Norma's version of hospice!" Nan announced to the three of us as she guided us to the livestock barns to see the baby goats. She and her daughter had come to meet us at the fair.

I had to laugh. Nothing about this past year was typical, so why would this be? All we could do was keep living in the moment and saying "Yes" to what life offered us, for however long that might be.

Later that evening I wondered if Norma had had the same reaction as Tim and I after seeing the Toyota MR2 outside the hospital.

"Did you see that car outside the hospital today?" I asked her.

"Oh, that was really strange. I thought Leo was coming to pick me up," Norma confided. "I didn't know what to think."

So she had felt it too, I thought. My eyes moistened and I gave her a little smile, emotionally moved to imagine Leo waiting for

her when she was ready to go, and sad to realize that she probably would be leaving us soon.

◊ ◊ ◊

Our experience with Hospice Care of the Northwest, which
was located on the mainland, and with island-based Hospice of
San Juan was wonderful, if not a bit overwhelming. There were
so many people involved in Norma's care, and *our* care too. Everyone had clearly done this before. But it did not take long for
Norma to show her new hospice nurse, Kathryn, that this was
no ordinary old lady she was caring for.

"I'm going to check your blood pressure, Norma," Kathryn
said while visiting us in the motor home for the first time. As
Norma sat comfortably in her Euro-chair, sipping on her cup
of afternoon tea, Kathryn also attached an oxygen meter to her
middle finger and then listened to her heart and lungs through
a stethoscope she retrieved from her medical bag. "Can I slide
your slippers off, Norma?" she ventured.

Norma's twinkling eyes met mine as the first slipper was removed from her swollen foot. We both knew what Kathryn
was going to find and we began to chuckle. Tim's laughter soon
followed when he saw what was happening. With the slipper off,
Kathryn was surprised to see that Norma's toes had bright pink
flowers painted on them. She had recently received a pedicure,
and actually this was the first time her toenails had ever donned
polish. Norma was beaming as Kathryn fawned over her fanci-
ful adornment.

Then came an inspection of Norma's feet and ankles. Kathryn's
hands moved skillfully over her paper-thin skin but stopped

abruptly just above the ankle. "What's up with your skin here?" she asked with concern. "What is this discoloration on your legs? What is this line?"

Norma's smile broadened as she proudly replied, "Well, that's my tan line. My socks usually go right to here."

"I can tell I have something to learn from you, Norma." Kathryn laughed.

◊ ◊ ◊

We thought that all the decisions had been made and that all the hard conversations were out of the way. That first week on San Juan Island, when we saw how quickly Norma was fading, we decided to have her complete a "Five Wishes" directive. I had discovered this document at an information kiosk at the hospital where Leo had spent his final days the previous summer. It was a living will that considered a person's personal, emotional, and spiritual needs as well as that person's medical wishes, and when signed in front of two witnesses, it became a legal document recognized in all but eight states. One of the few questions that Norma filled in was "How do you want people to remember you?" In her shaky hand, she wrote: "She was a nice person." As difficult as it was to have this talk, we felt confident afterward that we knew how best to meet all of Norma's needs.

With the Five Wishes filled out and our hospice team in place, we thought we would agree completely with all their recommendations and that Norma would soon die in her sleep like her mother had, which was, she told me, her hope. "The day Granny died she had lunch with her friends in the nursing home dining room," she had said months ago. "After lunch, she made her way back to her room for a nap and never woke up. That was it. That sounds pretty good to me."

Instead, things only got more intense.

The hospice doctor had recommended that Norma take Lasix, a very strong diuretic that treated fluid retention and the swelling caused by congestive heart failure. Its use, however, caused a lot of problems for Norma. It induced a dozen or so trips to the toilet during the day and another half dozen at night. The side effects were numerous and included constipation and a potassium loss that required her to take more medications to compensate. We were all beginning to be exhausted with the process by now. Norma ditched the torturous compression socks that were prescribed to help with her leg swelling, and once she had reduced her fluid intake, she ditched the diuretic too. She hated it.

It did not take long for the fluid to come back after she ceased taking the pills, and on her next visit Kathryn told us that the hospice physician said it was time to resume the regimen. None of us was sure to what end, though. Norma's ninety-one-year-old body was obviously failing her; her decline was visibly clear and steep. Were we torturing her with these medications for a limited outcome? "I just want to rest," she would say, exhausted by yet another trip to the bathroom.

"Help me to understand why she needs the Lasix again," Tim insisted during our next conversation with our hospice nurse.

"It will help her to breathe," she answered, insinuating that of course breathing was in her best interest.

Tim was not so easily convinced. "To what end are we prolonging her life?" he queried. "Where is the quality?"

The conversation seemed to go in circles. Norma drifted off to sleep and Tim disengaged from the discussion, feeling misunderstood.

"But it will help her breathe," Kathryn said again in a low voice and just to me.

"Help me understand how this drug works long term," I said, seeking to comprehend how much more time Norma might get in return for its miserable side effects.

Kathryn was very patient with me. Tim sat at the dinette and listened without participation as she and I talked through the various ways Norma could die, what symptoms we could expect, and how we could support her experience.

"Phew. It is rare that I speak this frankly with families," Kathryn said. She sounded like an overachieving teenager breaking the news to her parents that she had just gotten a B on her report card and was unsure how they would react. "It is more refreshing than you can imagine," she added.

Kathryn was now the second nurse to say that to us, but it still did not sink in.

"I'm surprised to hear that," I replied, assuming that many other families had it more together than we did. "I would think this was an everyday conversation by the time someone reached hospice."

At the end of Kathryn's visit, I was committed to talking to Norma about taking the Lasix again without any input from Tim or anyone else. Just us.

The next day, I had a quiet moment with Norma while Tim was outside with Ringo. We talked about her "ticker" and how it probably did not have too many "ticks" left. I reiterated what the nurse shared with us about the fluid building in her lungs and how that would lead to her death sooner than later. If she wanted to start the Lasix treatment again, we could clear out her lungs for a while. It would probably make her breathing easier and give her a couple more weeks.

Eventually it would catch up to her and she would transition soon either way.

"I understand," she said with clear eyes and remarkable lucidity, reaching for my left hand.

In the same moment, my right hand ran along her thick, fluid-filled leg. "The question I need you to think about," I continued, "is if you want to take the Lasix again for a few days to relieve some of this fluid you are retaining."

I could see Norma trying to form the right words with her mouth.

I quickly went on, "I don't want you to answer right now. I hope you will think about it and pray about it. This is your life and your decision. No matter what you decide, we will honor you. Everyone will be okay. Either way you decide, we have the medicine to make sure you are comfortable enough to gently and peacefully pass."

She was silent.

"Timmy will be okay," I said.

Her eyes gently closed.

"I'll be okay. Heck, Ringo will be okay too."

More time passed in silence.

"We'll talk about it again tomorrow," I told her.

Her eyes opened. "Okay." She was her old stoic self.

"Norma, you are the bravest person I know," I told her. "I used to think Stacy was, but I have changed my mind, I think it is—"

Before I could finish, she looked me in the eye and whispered, "I'm sipping 'Stacy water.'"

I knew exactly what she meant. She was summoning strength from the closest thing any of us had to a guardian angel or a superhero.

My gaze held on her cloudy blue eyes for a few moments. I could tell that clarity had arrived. She was preparing herself for a magnificent transition. If Stacy could do it, so could Norma.

I whispered back, "I'd like to know where to find some of that 'Stacy water.' Can you give me a hint?"

While beginning to doze off to sleep, she had just enough energy to say, "You'll have to find it for yourself."

The next thing I knew, it was time for another dreaded trip to the toilet. Singing in my best nursery rhyme voice "Put one foot in front of the other," we slowly made it to the bathroom, cracking up with laughter.

The "Stacy water" was working for us both.

That night at nine o'clock sharp, the three of us began our routine of moving her from the front of the motor home to her queen suite in the back. Tim and I helped her out of her chair and untangled the long oxygen hose so she would not run over it with her walker. Ringo moved from his spot under the foot of her bed to his nest in the front of the motor home.

The song for the night was our rendition of the 1958 Latin hit "Tequila" by the Champs. Each step brought a smile to her face. By the time we made it to the sliding door that divided our nighttime spaces, her hips were shaking to the rhythm of Tim's thigh-slapping drumbeats. The three of us were buckled over in laughter.

"If we weren't laughing, we'd be crying!" Norma declared between breaths.

Truer words were never spoken.

We were up twice that night, helping Norma back and forth from the toilet, managing adult briefs, oxygen tubes, and legs that were less steady every time they were called upon for use.

◊ ◊ ◊

The next morning, over a Dungeness-crab omelet that Tim served up for breakfast, I had a chance to talk to Norma again about the decision she was tasked with making. "Remember what we talked about yesterday, about the Lasix and the fluid in your legs and lungs?"

"Yes, sure I do. I don't want to do Lasix," she said matter-of-factly. Before we could continue, a hospice home-health aide arrived to bathe her.

"I want to talk a little bit more after your shower, okay?" I said as the bathroom door closed. It was important to me that she completely understood that her condition was declining and she might die sooner if she did not take the Lasix. I also wanted her to know that we supported her decision either way.

Twenty-four hours after the awkward conversation with Kathryn, I was back on the phone with her. "The doctor wants to put her back on Lasix for three days," she said. "Then we would switch to another drug for . . ." I desperately tried to follow along and write down all the details of the plan the doctor had devised. Kathryn was beginning to sound a little like Charlie Brown's teacher to me—nothing but undistinguishable words. She finished outlining each step and then offered, "Or we could not do the Lasix." Her tone of voice told me that was the wrong answer.

But I had seen the look in Norma's eyes, and I was now sipping "Stacy water" too. A surge of courage and certainty rose within me. "Kathryn, we have spent every minute of every day with Norma since last June when Leo fell ill," I said. "We are confident that the amount of love and joy Norma has experienced in her last year of life is a rare occurrence, especially for someone of her age."

"It sure is," she agreed.

"We have no regrets, nothing left unsaid or undone. If she did have a bucket list, there is nothing left to check off. It has been her desire all along to die a natural death, not dealing with the side effects of medications or being hooked up to artificial means. The oxygen support was a stretch she eventually agreed to. This is who she is. She is at peace.

"I will talk to her once more to make sure," I continued, "but I'm pretty confident that we are leaning in the direction of no more miserable medications. This is not Tim's agenda or mine; it is Tim and me honoring what we know is important to his mom. Please understand."

And, much to her credit, Kathryn did understand. Any fears I had had that she might be judging us or questioning our motives dissipated after that call. From then on, she became one of the family.

Tim and I were outside cracking hazelnuts and chatting when, after Norma's shower, she came to stand at the motor home's front door, cane in hand. "Can I come out?" she inquired. From his spot under the picnic table, Ringo lifted his head and wagged his tail. His buddy had not been interested in venturing outside for over a week. Her request surprised us too. We spotted her as she hobbled down the steps with her twisted white-oak cane in one hand, her other grasping tightly to the motor home's handrails.

The discussion I had promised myself I would have with Norma came about organically. We discussed the pros and cons of her different options. We talked about the fact that her life was coming to a close and that one option may allow her to live a couple of weeks longer than the other. "This is your life and your decision," I reiterated. "Tim and I will support you no matter what. Do you understand what I am asking?"

"Yes, I do. I don't want to do the Lasix. What do you think?" She looked at me first.

"It doesn't matter what I think," I reiterated.

Norma slowly turned her head so that she was directly facing her son. "Timmy, is that okay? What do you think?" I could hear the concern in her voice. She was asking Tim if he was okay with her choice to die sooner rather than later.

"Mom, it is your decision. If you are asking what I think of your decision, I think it is a fine one. We will make sure you are comfortable. I love you, Mama."

"Okay, I say no Lasix," Norma declared.

After a few hours of sunshine therapy, the clouds rolled in and Norma climbed her way back into the motor home. We chatted and joked as I helped Norma into her chair and got her some-thing sweet to eat. In the middle of licking an orange popsicle she stopped, spontaneously looked up to the heavens, and said, "Lord, expect all of us up there some day, even the goofy ones around here." Her laugh lit up the otherwise dim confines of the motor home on this now rainy day. Her twinkling eyes meeting ours, the "goofy ones."

That night we sang "When the Saints Go Marching In" as Tim spun Norma's wheelchair around in a tight circle and she wiggled her bottom in the seat, her hands leading the march. A blanket of relief had draped over us. There would be no more agonizing over decisions. We could just love one another and say good-bye.

◊ ◊ ◊

With each trip to the bathroom, Norma's legs worked less and less on their own. We had to trade her walker in for the wheelchair to transport her the twenty-five feet to the toilet in the rear of the motor home. At night she started using adult diapers—briefs, they are called, under the veil of dignity—and we were all getting more and more comfortable with what only a short time ago had been taboo. Norma's dignity was slowly being taken away as hard as we tried to keep it intact for the duration of her life.

Once, when her pants were soiled, she said, "Oh my!" surprised by the bodily functions that were deserting her.

Instead of comforting her this time and telling her that everything was okay, I proclaimed, "Well, shit happens!" I could see that my conversational filter was eroding quickly.

Before I could process what I had just said to my mother-in-law, Norma laughed and said, "Shit happens! Ain't that the truth!"

◊ ◊ ◊

I found myself constantly thinking *Norma would love this* and *I have to show Norma that.*

We understood that she would never walk down the steps of the motor home again. Her old legs had gone on strike and the rest of her body was following closely behind. Yet I could not help myself from wanting to show her all that I saw and enjoyed in the everyday world.

Our Baja California friend Mark came again to visit on San Juan Island to offer us his support. He and I were out picking hazelnuts in Steve's orchard when a tiny, brilliant-green frog jumped onto my hand. "I have to show Norma!" I exclaimed to Mark. I dropped everything else and hurried to the motor home, all the while trying to minimize the trauma the frog was experiencing. Once I made it to Norma's chair, the iridescent amphibian jumped out of my hand straight into Norma's. If there was any question whether Norma was still alive, we got our answer; she about jumped out of her skin when it landed in her hand, but then she could not get enough of little "Freddy the Frog" before he leaped out of her hands and out the front door.

We began to feel a crispness in the air we had not experienced for a very long time. Everything seemed to be in transition. I ran errands in town with Nan one afternoon and was struck by the fact that the leaves were already beginning to change color. One young oak tree in the grocery store parking lot particularly stood out; its leaves were a brilliant red and each leaf seemed larger than Norma's head. "I have to pick a few to take back to Norma," I said, making a mental note to do so when we returned to the car. Instead, while I was in line I answered a call from our hospice nurse. I walked away from my groceries on the conveyor belt and forgot all about the oak leaves.

My brain felt as though it were constantly changing channels. I had trouble remembering things and I struggled to be articulate. It was as though the signature fog of the Pacific Northwest had moved into my head with a long-term lease. Nan had been a caregiver for both her mom and her mother-in-law, and I asked her if I would ever return to a higher level of functioning. "Yes," she assured me. "This is all part of it."

I had barely looked at myself in the mirror during the past few weeks. When I caught a glimpse, I noticed unbrushed hair, unfamiliar bags under my eyes, and newly formed wrinkles. Another reminder that I would never be the same either.

◊ ◊ ◊

We settled into a chaotic, sleep-deprived routine of bathroom assistance, pain management, and sleep-support medication as first Norma's left leg and then her right stopped working completely and getting up at all became very difficult. Her ability to speak was following closely behind.

Our bedtime rituals became more and more tender. We would hold hands and sit close together on Norma's bed, and while cloaked in the quiet stillness of night, we would say everything that was in our hearts to say. Nan and Steve began to join us in our bedtime music routine. They would play old-time songs and lullabies on their ukuleles, and we would all sing along. Norma still recalled her favorites, and her weak voice would join ours. One evening, when they asked again if Norma wanted them to play and sing, Tim said, "Not tonight. I think she is done," and he gently thanked them.

That same evening, Tim and I sat with Norma and quietly thanked her for just being who she was. We told her that her next adventure would be as grand as the one we had just shared. We reminded her that when we had all left Michigan together the year before, she had not known how this journey with us would turn out, but she had trusted it anyway. "We hope you can trust the next unknown adventure too," I softly said to her.

We administered her liquid pain medicine with a dropper and with great care. She usually fell into a deep sleep shortly after we did so, and so we said our good nights, I love yous, and good-byes just in case. Nothing was left unsaid. We had her imagine that she was going to zoom into heaven in Mister 2, or maybe float in on a hot-air balloon. Either one seemed fine with her since she smiled faintly and then drifted off into a dopey slumber. Before leaving her bedroom, Tim opened a nearby window to allow the angels in to escort her beautiful soul.

Tim and I settled in the front of the motor home and turned on the television for some distraction. The better part of an hour passed when Tim heard her uncharacteristically call out something unintelligible.

"What, Mama?" he blurted as he reached her bed at lightning speed. "Do you need something, Mom?"

We struggled to understand what she was trying to tell us, her mouth and vocal cords no longer able to communicate well. Not wanting to make her feel bad, I said, "I'm sorry, Norma, I'm having a hard time understanding what you are saying. Can you say it again?" We were very solemn and stressed by the prospect that she had something very important to tell us. Her lack of speech made it a frustrating exercise. Each time I asked a question, it felt worse.

Suddenly it dawned on me that our relationship had so often been based on humor. When we did not know what we were doing, we always found a way to laugh about it. Shit happens, right? I shifted from my serious voice into my smart-aleck tone. "I know what you want!" I declared.

Norma's tired eyes seemed to say, *God, I hope so. I cannot play this game much longer.*

"You want me to *sing*!" I sarcastically exclaimed.

To my absolute shock, she nodded her head in the affirmative.

"Really?!"

Again she nodded.

So I sang. I sang and sang and sang—more than a dozen songs. I sang the old-time tunes she knew the words to, the ones that just two nights before she was able to sing along with. I sang "When the Saints Go Marching In" and "Oh, Susannah." I sang "The Battle Hymn of the Republic" and "He's Got the Whole World in His Hands."

When I was sure she had had her fill of my terribly off-key voice, I asked her, "Is that enough?"

She shook her head again, but this time it was side to side.

"Do you want me to keep singing, Norma?"

She nodded again in the affirmative. Incredulous, I asked one more time. The answer was still the same.

So I kept singing. I sang "A Bicycle Built for Two" and "Go Tell It on the Mountain." Then I sang one of our favorites, "This Little Light of Mine." She finally and gently drifted off to sleep.

She slept for three more days and I sang for three more nights. On the fourth day she took her last sip of "Stacy water."

CHAPTER 16

Rest

BAJA CALIFORNIA, MEXICO

NOVEMBER AND BEYOND

[Tim]

Ramie and I both realized early on in our trip that my mom would not be ready to join us on our usual pilgrimage to Baja California during our first winter together. The lack of amenities and the cultural divide would have been a difficult transition right out of the gate for her. Instead, we spent three wonderful months in sunny Florida.

Then, sometime in early spring as we were touring the Eastern Seaboard, Mom said she would like to go to Mexico with us the next time around. Perhaps her change of heart was from meeting many of our Baja California friends along our journey; maybe it was seeing the whale sharks in Atlanta and wanting to see them in their natural environment; or maybe it was because she knew the Baja felt like home to us and she wanted to know what that meant.

Aware that I could not possibly make Mom comfortable enough at our usual spot on a primitive beach, I arranged to rent a small house at nearby Posada Concepcion. It would provide first-world amenities, such as running water, flush toilets, and electricity for twelve hours a day from the small community's diesel generator—creature comforts that I knew she would need to be at ease. We also made sure to pick up her passport when we visited her Presque Isle home in July.

After all the plans were set, I eagerly anticipated the time when Mom would actually go to the beach with us. I often fantasized about how fun it would be to get her on one of our paddleboards. I understood that she was too old and unsteady to stand on it, so instead I imagined her tiny body resting on its wide deck while relaxing with her feet dangling over the side. There would be that now-famous smile opening her face as she bobbed on the crystal-clear waters of the Bay of Conception. Later in the day I would make her my signature margarita, using damiana liqueur instead of triple sec, and we would toast to the journey thus far. We would sit outside on the porch until the sun set behind the mountains and enjoy another ordinary moment in an extraordinary life.

Instead, Mom's ashes were sealed in an urn tucked neatly and securely under her former bed as Ramie and I drove the motor home south down the western edge of the United States. Ringo, who had climbed into the mortuary van with Mom's body and would not get out when it was time to drive away, continued to curl up at the foot of her bed at night, his grief palpable to us. We were on a different adventure now: learning how to travel with our heartache and how to break camp and move on down the road without her.

After storing the motor home in California for the winter, we continued our journey south of the border in our Jeep Wrangler. With so much to do before we could go, we had been forced to leave Mom's possessions just as they were in the motor home, resolving to deal with them when we returned the following spring. But there was one drawer we had not been able to leave untouched: Mom's "squirrel drawer."

Whenever Mom had received souvenirs, small gifts, or tokens of affection, she went to her room and hid them away for future viewing, much like a squirrel would do with its acorns. It became a joke among the three of us. If we asked her where something important was, she would say, "I probably put it in my squirrel drawer." A giggle always followed whenever she uttered the clever name for her secret hiding place. It contained all of Mom's treasures. A lapel pin and wristband from the Hilton Head Island Saint Patrick's Day Parade; a piece of rose quartz she had received as a gift in South Dakota; perfect seashells culled from Sanibel Island, Florida; and a miniature L.L.Bean–boot key chain were among the many items that crowded the drawer.

In one corner we found the Norma Melon Head doll made by Dwight, a maintenance worker at a campground we had stayed at in Florida. Visiting us one evening as his alter ego "Mr. Jamaica," he gave her the rustic wooden doll made in her likeness, complete with curly strands of hair made from grey yarn, as a token of his affection. It was the last night of our three-week visit there, and he had asked me earlier if he could share with Mom a song he had written for her. As he entered our motor home that night, we all were shocked when we saw his dreadlocks. Usually tucked neatly under the large black knit cap he always wore on the job, they were long enough to touch our carpeted floor. He sat on the couch across from Mom and strummed his guitar, singing reggae songs to her as if Ramie and I were not there. "Your journey has touched my heart. Thank you," he had told her before he left.

Near the bottom of Mom's squirrel drawer we found a large round pin featuring images of Mickey Mouse and Goofy and the words "First Visit." How could we forget her first visit to the Epcot theme park at the Walt Disney World Resort that January? I remembered spending the whole day pushing her wheelchair through the attraction that is often referred to as a "permanent world's fair." It was divided into two sections: Future World, consisting of eight pavilions, and World Showcase, which was themed to eleven world nations.

At the end of the Spaceship Earth ride, Mom and I created a cartoon video that featured photographs of our faces on the two main characters. It showed us cruising around in a futuristic flying saucer that could also become a submersible craft. Although it had no audio, we posted it on Mom's Facebook page to the delight of many of her followers who wanted to see her in video format. Ramie and I still laugh at all the Internet and print articles we saw that stated we not only were traveling the United States but had taken my mom to Germany and China as well. The Disney people apparently had made a convincing international backdrop for us to have fooled so many people.

In a small velvet bag under some children's drawings, we found the true mother lode: three small vials containing tiny nuggets of gold suspended in water. Ramie and I noticed that two of the vials were ours and had somehow gotten "squirrelled" away in Mom's drawer.

"I wondered where mine ended up!" Ramie laughed.

We fondly remembered the day that we all had panned for those specimens at the Consolidated Gold Mine in Dahlonega, Georgia, sometime in early April. We had accepted an invitation from the mine's general manager, Dathan, to take a personal underground tour and to try our luck gold panning. I will never forget Mom's resolve and determination to walk all of the inclines and steps that faced us on our half-mile trek. Even as we descended to over three hundred feet below the surface, Mom was not fazed, only sitting occasionally on the folding chair that Dathan had so thoughtfully carried along. Mom was a true rock hound, and that experience in the mine reminded me of the times our family had spent weekend afternoons searching for fossils at a local limestone quarry when I was a child.

We also found a small spiral-bound notebook that had served as Mom's journal. Inside were page upon page of delicately handwritten notes about our journey together. Ramie and I had seen her scribbling in it with her pencil throughout our trip, but we had never peeked in it, nor did she ever offer to share. Just seeing her familiar handwriting left me sad and wanting to cry.

"Let's save this to read down in the Baja," Ramie suggested, our loss too recent. I had to agree.

We placed the journal in a safe spot before continuing our drive south.

◊ ◊ ◊

We crossed the U.S.-Mexico border early that Tuesday, anxious to get some miles behind us as we followed Mexico Highway 1 south to our winter home on the Sea of Cortez. Nearly eight hundred miles long, the Baja California Peninsula is the earth's second longest, and we were going to be driving over three-fourths of it to reach our destination. The shoulderless, two-lane road offered stunning vistas at nearly every turn as it drunkenly wound along the sides of the mountains and dead volcanoes that form the peninsula's spine.

As we slowed down to roll over the *topes*—speed bumps—that appeared at the entrance and exit of each tiny village we passed through, I wondered what Mom might have thought of what was outside the window. Would she have felt sorry for the poor people begging on the side of the road? Would she have wanted to stop and give them some pesos? Would all the new sights, sounds, and smells have been too overwhelming for her? I would never know.

The Vizcaino Desert was the last stretch of high plateau we drove before descending to the peninsula's eastern coast. We had to proceed slowly through the copper-mining town of Santa Rosalia, which was still recovering from a recent hurricane. We dodged huge potholes as we passed by crumpled vehicles still buried in the rubble of a landslide. We were now approaching the home stretch to our slice of paradise.

The little fishing village of Mulegé is the closest thing to civilization near our beach home. Over the years, Ramie and I have established relationships with many of its 3,200 residents, some of whom we are honored to call friends. On our way down we always stop here for supplies before driving the final miles to the Bay of Conception, and today was no exception. A large *tope* in front of Mario's taco stand made it easy to stop and make the left turn into his dusty parking lot. We reacquainted with Mario and enjoyed a plate of tacos made from the fish he had caught earlier that morning. As we sat under a giant ficus tree that shaded the two outside tables, a heavy sadness tugged on my heart. "Mom would have loved this," I said to Ramie as I crunched on the fresh radishes on my plate. Ramie just reached out and touched my hand as together we took a deep breath.

Rolling down the village's main street, we came upon Adolfo, sweeping the sidewalk outside his family's curio shop. He beamed once he recognized us in our new Jeep and waved with a toothy smile. "*Hola, amigos,*" he yelled. "What color? How many? Almost free!"

It felt good to be back and driving the narrow, confusing one-way streets. We pulled in the Jeep's mirrors for good measure.

As usual, it took a visit to almost every shop to buy everything we needed. My grasp of the Spanish language was quickly returning as I greeted and talked to the cashiers and to people we met on the street.

After filling some five-gallon bottles with potable water, we continued south. Even though I had been visiting this area since the mid-1990s, I was once again struck by the view as we crested the hill and, for the first time, could see the entire Bay of Conception stretched out before us. Scalloped bays with white sandy beaches line the entire western shore, and a half dozen small islands dot its turquoise waters. It truly is a breath-taking sight.

We parked the Wrangler outside the green stucco *casita*—just steps from the water—that was to be our winter home. We entered through the sliding glass door and looked around. The weight of Mom's absence loomed large as our eyes scanned the two bedrooms and glanced at the accessible shower. Now that we were here, we realized this was much more space than we needed. The second bedroom, the one meant for Mom, had bunk beds. Ramie and I laughed, imagining Mom climbing onto the top bunk just because it was there. I made my way up the ladder and lay down on the single mattress, a flood of memories of the past year racing through my brain.

"I still can't believe we got her on that zip line," I said within earshot of Ramie as I imagined my mom zipping down from the top bunk into her adjacent bright yellow bathroom. I was remembering the time in North Carolina when she rode my old friend Kevin's homemade contraption that had been suspended high in two trees. "And it was all caught on video by the *Today* show cameras. Unbelievable!"

"That was the same day as her first horseback ride," Ramie remembered. "I will never forget when her guides told her to sit up straight in the saddle and to push her shoulders back."

"No kidding," I retorted. Both of us recalled how we almost yelled *"She can't straighten her back!"* across the riding arena, when somehow she did. My cheeks were wet again as I thought about that accomplishment. Tears could still flow for almost any reason now.

We both agreed that Mom would have loved the seashell art hanging on the walls, the tropical fish decorations and having a real flushing toilet. She would have held court on either of the two outdoor patios, likely enjoying the admiration of former strangers, who, whether they knew it or not, would soon be touched deeply by her zeal for life. She also would have collected many more items to put in that squirrel drawer of hers.

◊ ◊ ◊

The neighborhood was new to us, and our true comfort zone was a couple of miles farther south, on a beach with no houses. We hoped we would fit into the bricks-and-mortar community here as well as we had the camping beach we had frequented for these many years. Only time would tell.

While sleeping that first night in a strange bed, Mom, Dad, and Stacy showed up in one of my dreams. They were all flying around together, and Stacy was the only one to speak. "Hey, Timmy, check this out," she said to me in a voice I recognized. "Dad and I have already got Mom flying too. She was a quick study!" My family all appeared so happy until I, as I often do in my dreams, spontaneously started flying too. "What's this?" Stacy asked in an angry tone. "I thought this flying thing was only for us dead folks." We continued to fly together for a short time before the three of them disappeared into the ether. I was filled up with more love than I had ever felt possible when I awoke from my vivid dream. As I heard the waves gently lapping on the shore through the open window, the clarity I received was inspiring. I understood that the veil between our worlds was very thin and the energy of those we love was never far. I knew that I would be able to work through my grief.

◊ ◊ ◊

We have always found peace in our morning routine in the Baja. Rising before dawn to paddle kayaks toward the sunrise was an everyday occurrence we were ready to reestablish. Ramie's discipline in this practice inspired me to follow suit on our first morning. By eight o'clock we had already paddled around an island a little more than a mile offshore when we briefly stopped to watch an osprey dive for breakfast. The water was calm and bright gold as the sun made its way over the mountains that form the peninsula on the eastern edge of the bay. Three dolphins swam by but did not stay long. The rain and fog of the Pacific Northwest were now a distant memory.

And then we heard it. The sound of bagpipes. "Amazing Grace" was vibrating across the smooth water. We both stopped paddling our kayaks and began to weep. We wept for the full five minutes of the song, knowing that it was Garry broadcasting from a loudspeaker in front of his palm-frond *palapa*. He played this beautiful rendition daily before he reported the weather and tides on his shortwave radio. This day it felt like he was playing it for us and only us.

Our exhilarating morning paddle was followed by a quick breakfast of fresh homemade *tamales* Luli had brought by, which she covers with a warm, moist towel to keep fresh. Next we took Ringo for a long walk up the Good Heart Trail across Mexico Highway 1 from our little house. From the top of the trail we could see many nearby bays and the camping beaches, mostly empty this early in the season. We were excited to reconnect with our people, who would be steadily rolling in over the next days, weeks, and months.

Day one of our new routine felt good. It was a relief to know that things were starting to—could start to—go back to normal. And yet I also knew that things would never be the same again. We had just had the most amazing year of our lives. What would it look like to move on after such a transformative year, after the loss of my mom, whom I had only just gotten the chance to know—really know? I could not help but wonder. Would I feel the serenity I had felt after my dream with Mom, Dad, and Stacy, and would I remember that I did not need to have everything figured out? I eventually realized I only needed to live for today, just as Mom had.

The afternoon was getting hot, so Ramie's first order of business was to "swim the blue," as our dear friend Glenna says. Glenna, a Canadian nearing eighty years old, never misses a chance to swim in the perfect waters of the Bay of Conception. She had inspired Ramie to do the same over the years.

While the water was Ramie's first priority, mine was to hang our hammock up on the south side of our house. When Ramie returned from her swim she crawled into the oversize hammock next to me. Her cool body against mine felt refreshing in the late afternoon heat. The ups and downs of the past year had hit us both, and we were exhausted. With Ringo cooling his belly on the stone patio below us, we all drifted off to sleep until dinnertime. Finally we took the deep breath we had all been waiting to take.

◊ ◊ ◊

After a few more weeks of this routine, catching up with friends, and napping—lots of napping—we were ready to dive into Mom's journal. By now Nan and Steve, as well as Mark, had arrived at the beach, and we invited them to join us at our *casita* one evening for dinner. It would be just the five of us who had been there in Friday Harbor at the end of Mom's life. Now a tight group bonded by an unimaginable life experience, we were all ready to reminisce about Mom by reading her journal aloud while we ate fish tacos and sipped margaritas.

Flipping through the notebook's pages, Ramie started the journal reading. I leaned back in my chair as she shared an entry.

Sunday, November 29. Kind of cloudy today. Went into town to the World War II Museum. They greeted me like they

knew me all my life. Shook hands with all kinds of people.
Thanking me for being in the service.

"I had a feeling our visit to the World War Two Museum in New Orleans was the first time your mom felt valued for her military service," Ramie said after reading the passage.

That rang true to me since I had never seen her more proud as I had that day. She had been part of a fading generation of veterans who rarely sought validation for their sacrifices in that war.

It was my turn next. I flipped through a couple of pages, scanning for something that spoke to me. I read:

Friday, March 4. Had a rainstorm last night, thunder and
lightning. Today cold and wet. Only 51° this morning.
Went for my walk. Tim and Ramie decided they wanted a
hamburger for dinner so we went to a local restaurant. Met the
owner of the place, called Big George. A big black dude, very
nice. Had pictures taken. I also got an orchid on my plate.
I had asparagus and crab and mushrooms. Very good. For
dessert we had chocolate caramel cake. There was no charge!
I asked Tim, "I bet you are glad you brought me along now,
aren't you?!"

We all busted out in laughter.

"I can't believe how she described Big George," Nan said.

Heads nodded all around the circle as our laughing continued.

And then I homed in on the second to last line. "Mom loved her 'freebies,' that's for sure!" I said. "She also loved to use that line about being glad we brought her along," I remembered, smiling as I thought back on all the times I had heard her say it.

Clockwise, we passed the blue spiral-bound notebook from person to person. Nan paused for a few moments, reading an entry to herself, and then gave a joyful laugh as she shared it with the rest of us.

> *Tuesday, March 22. Cold and sunny. Going to Charleston today and staying till Thursday. Took about two hours to get to Charleston. We are staying at the best hotel in town. I am in the P R E S I D E N T I A L   S W E E T. A living room with a dining table that seats from 8 to 12 people. A wet bar, half bath, bedroom, dressing room, and bathroom with shower and bathtub. Ramie and Tim are down the hall in their own room with Ringo. Had a glass of champagne when we got there. We are always eating.*

"I love the way she spelled 'sweet,' " Nan said.

Mom clearly had been impressed by the hotel accommodations we enjoyed while visiting the "Holy City." I did not know if that was an intentional play on words by my mom, but I had to chuckle nonetheless.

Nan passed the journal to Steve, who read:

> *Sunday, May 15. Cloudy and cold today. Moving on today to L.L. Bean parking lot. Changed our mind and went to a campground instead so we could dump and do some laundry. Got a police escort out of town with lights and siren. Lots of neighbors came to see us off.*

"Wait. I have to read the next one too," he said as a certain word in it caught his eye.

> *Monday, May 16. Cold today—up in Maine, Freeport.*
> *Going to move to L.L. Bean parking lot, I think. Went to*
> *L.L. Bean's and I did some shopping. Got a new jacket, pair*
> *of tan pants, and a new shirt for Mexico. Went back to the*
> *campground. Too cold to take a walk outside.*

"She really was looking forward to coming down to the Baja," I said, holding back tears. "Marky, it's your turn." I took the book from Steve and quickly passed it to Mark, trying to maintain my composure.

Mark cleared his throat and dramatically feathered the pages. "Ah-hum," he started.

> *Sunday, September 27. Calm today. We went into Boulder*
> *and met Suzanne and then went to the Celestial Tea Co. Took*
> *a tour through the place, very nice. Ramie took my picture*
> *with the big stuffed bear. Had a tour through Boulder with*
> *Tim pushing me in the wheelchair. Stopped in a Pot Shop. No*
> *kidding! Got some cream for my leg and then came back.*

Laughter filled the small living room.

"She cracks me up! I wonder if she ever mentions the use of marijuana anywhere else in here," Ramie interjected.

My mind drifted back to that autumn day in the Colorado Rockies when any boundaries between us were starting to break down.

Mom's journal was not long-winded because she never was. The notebook held simple sentences describing the day and was sprinkled with a few reflections. She charted our time from getting stuck at the Mackinac Bridge to her first pedicure with polish, from touching a moon rock at the Kennedy Space Center to how she stayed up late to watch the end of the Super Bowl eating hot wings and shrimp cocktail.

As we continued to read, we laughed, cried, and reminisced about the big things she had chronicled, like the hot-air balloon ride, and about the small things—just a note about the weather or that she read her book all day or that Ringo rested his chin on her lap when we went for a drive in the mountains.

There were plenty of days during the past year when we had wondered if we were doing enough for Mom. Some days had been very exciting, sure, but others had not been terribly interesting. Reading her journal, we could see how much joy she had found in the little things: hairdos and visitors, seeing a bunny on the road, completing a jigsaw puzzle with Ramie, or picking up new postcards to mail back home.

Ramie looked down at the journal and read another entry. "Remember this, Timmy? This was 'Lobstergram Day.'"

Tuesday, May 24. Partly sunny 58°. Tim and Ramie went for a long walk. And they came back and I went for a walk around here. Before dinner Tim made a nice fire while he fixed a lobster for dinner.

I flashed on Dad's last days and quickly realized that anything we had done for Mom was one hundred times better than what he had experienced in the hospital. Going for a walk, sitting by the fire, and eating lobster on paper plates now sounded pretty great compared to that alternative.

"Wow, Timmy, listen to this," Ramie said when it was her turn again.

September 10. Cold as the aspen are turning yellow. Started out around 10 a.m. and went to Lake Jenny. Quite a few people so had to wait a while. Got a seat in the back of the boat. Took my hat off or I would've lost it in the wind. Nice guy told us all about the mountains surrounding the lake. When we got back we took a stroll along the lake and had lunch near the water. Went to Jackson Hole for groceries and headed for home. Saw a big bunch of bison and a few pronghorns. Everyone was kind of worn out so just sitting here and having a beer.

"I remember as early as September that she was already referring to the motor home and the campground as 'home,'" Ramie said thoughtfully. "I always hoped it felt like home to her."

It was Nan's turn. She picked up the journal and leafed through it a bit, stopping near the end. She read aloud:

Thursday, June 9. Sunny 58° cool. Got cold last night. We are going to Pittsburgh today. Patti came to pick us up. Saw a lot of different places. Went down & up the incline. Got some biscottis, caramel corn, ate lunch and came back. Around 8:00 p.m. Ringo got sick & Ramie & Tim had to take him to the vet. It was something about his stomach was twisted. Had to operate. Everything turned out fine. Stanley Cup was tonight.

"Are you kidding?!" Ramie shouted and looked at me. Neither of us could believe what we had just heard. All the entries so far perfectly aligned with our memories of those days. But not this one. "Did she really say everything was fine? There was nothing fine about that night." Ramie recounted to the group her version of that night, highlighting how different it was from

Mom's, sharing our sleepless night, our fear and anxiety, our dread.

Then she took the journal from Nan's hands and silently stared for a few moments at the page, Mom's entry about Ringo's surgery. "It's a perfect illustration of how she was much more equipped to take things in stride than we were," Ramie quietly said. "The truth is, in the end everything *was* fine. How did she know?"

A few moments later, Steve seemed to land on an entry he had been looking for. "Here it is," he said. "The other tree."

> *Friday, March 25. Today I got my hair cut. It needed it.*
> *In the afternoon went to Bluffton and met a lot of people,*
> *including the mayor and helped plant a red bud tree in Leo's*
> *honor. It was planted in a children's park and will have a*
> *plaque on it with Leo's name. This was in honor of all the*
> *trees Leo planted in his lifetime. Stopped at a shopping mall*
> *and got some new clothes.*

"Mom and her new clothes." I laughed. "She wasn't passing up an opportunity to update her style. We actually went shopping before the tree planting because she knew she would be on the evening news and wanted to look good."

"That was one of the most touching days of the trip," Ramie added. "That tree will be there forever, just like the Japanese maple we planted for Norma at her celebration of life with you guys at Overlook Park in Friday Harbor."

"It is so cool that the two trees span the entire country from South Carolina in the southeast to Washington in the northwest," Nan added, her comments warming the room. "They make up an arc of love, joy, and adventure that will be nurtured forever."

"Her energy lives on in these trees," Mark reflected, his connection with the natural world always front and center. "They will be a spiritual touchstone for so many."

"You know, you're right," I agreed. "There have already been people from all over visiting both of the trees. They send us photos and post them on their Facebook pages. People are looking after them. We have reports that they have both survived major storms in their young lives, and we even received a message from a nursing home worker from the UK who traveled to Bluffton's DuBois Park to visit Dad's tree while on vacation in the low country. Amazing. The breadth and depth of her story occasionally takes us aback. These trees will allow Mom's and Dad's spirits to live on, to have a landing place, like Marky said, a touchstone. We are so blown away and grateful for the love and hospitality we have received."

◊ ◊ ◊

When she was alive, my sister, Stacy, had a vision: She was going to retire at age fifty, buy a small horse farm outside Asheville, North Carolina, and have a home that included a guesthouse for Mom and Dad, complete with rocking chairs on the front porch. They would move in with her. She would take care of them. It was settled.

But Stacy did not make it. She died at age forty-four of tongue cancer.

More than anything, her death taught me that life is short. We can say these words again and again, but the idea does not necessarily sink in. The reality is, none of us knows how long—or short—our lives may be. Someone like my mom can be given a virtual death sentence only to be surprised when those days last longer than anyone ever expected. Someone else can put off life's joys, only to be struck down far too soon and long before those dreams ever materialize.

It's trite but true: all we have is the moment that is unfolding right now. And no matter where any of us are, that now can be filled with beauty, joy, love, and possibility. Mom was living proof of that.

Over the course of our Baja California stay, Ramie and I made it through the entire journal. In the end, the most remarkable thing we discovered about Mom's diary was not what was in it but rather what was missing. She did not write a single word about cancer or fame—the two big themes of the journey for us. She did not write about seeing herself on television or about being recognized on the street. She did not write about the fear of dying or illness at all. Instead, she talked about life, living, and the little things that brought her happiness: a sturdy wheelchair and someone to push her; the sight of mama and baby goats; cookies and peppermint patties; getting a good hair perm; the gift of a Santa hat and a new bar of soap; and food to enjoy along with family, friends, and her trusty sidekick, Ringo.

She certainly attracted what she focused on: joy begets joy, love begets love, and peace begets peace. In every smile, every goofy face, every stop on the map, we learned so much from her. I am so grateful that I did not rob myself of the opportunity to get to know my mom. Ultimately, she taught me to say *"Yes!"*

Acknowledgments

There are times in life when serendipity takes over.

Shortly after Colleen Martell's beloved grandmother passed away, our *Driving Miss Norma* Facebook page appeared in her life. Like many others, she sent a heartfelt note to share her grief with us. Her short message, however, would change our lives forever. Colleen has a gift for recognizing a good story, and she encouraged us to write ours down. She eventually became our editor, mentor, coach, and cheerleader while we penned our first book. She probably did not expect to also become our therapist and confidante, crying through the final chapters with us as Norma was simultaneously taking her final breaths. We so appreciate her for showing up in our lives.

We did not know what a literary agent really did until we were introduced to one of the finest. Stephanie Tade has served as our "Inspirer-in-Chief" throughout the book-writing process, and she convinced us that the world needed to read our simple story. As we ran through the streets of New York City with Stephanie from one publishing house to the next, we got a crash course about the book world, as well as a lesson on passion and trusting the process. Although we were to embark on something so totally foreign to us, we never doubted that the best agent in the world had our backs.

Thousands of people wrote to tell us that our story should be made into a book, but it was Julia Pastore from HarperOne who said, "They are right." Julia provided us with the confidence to put pen to paper, and her insight, compassion, and continual feedback during the writing process served as our lodestar. We thank her for this as well as her unwavering enthusiasm.

Without the aforementioned women, there would be no book. Without the hundreds of thousands of Miss Norma fans, there would be no story. The human connections we made through our Facebook page exceeded our wildest imaginations. We continue to receive messages of support, encouragement, and kindness, as well as an occasional invitation for cake and beer. During our highest moments, our new friends were flying with us, and when things got tough, they stayed by our side. The love we received from around the world has buoyed us beyond belief, and we are eternally grateful for it.

About the Authors

Like most people who find themselves caring for one or both of their elderly parents, Tim Bauerschmidt and Ramie Liddle were not experts in the field. Ramie was a high school counselor with a background in parks and recreation; Tim tabled his journalism degree to remodel homes. Later, they chose to embrace a nomadic lifestyle with Ringo, their Standard Poodle.

In 2011, the couple began sharing photos and stories about "life on the road" on their blog www.poodleinapod.blogspot .com. Ramie started the wildly popular Facebook page *Driving Miss Norma* after Tim's mom joined them in late August 2015. A few months later, the page went viral and now has over half a million followers from around the globe. Miss Norma's story has been covered by nearly every major news media outlet worldwide, and the book about her yearlong journey will be published in at least ten languages.

Ramie's passion for photography, her delight in reading maps, and her love for her mother-in-law allowed her to act as an embedded photojournalist, counselor, and logistics coordinator for the family's motor-home adventure. Tim's much appreciated talents for driving safely, for being able to fix things, and for preparing great-tasting food made the whole trip just that much better.

The couple still enjoys traveling, exploring the natural world, hiking, kayaking, paddleboarding, and sharing meals with friends and former strangers.